THE ATONEMENT

THE ATONEMENT

by
Gordon H. Clark

The Trinity Foundation
Jefferson, Maryland

Cover: Detail of *Crucifixion with the Virgin,
Sts. John, Jerome and Mary Magdalene*
Pietro Perugino
Andrew W. Mellon Collection
National Gallery of Art
Washington, D.C.

The Atonement
©1987 The Trinity Foundation
Post Office Box 169
Jefferson, Maryland 21755
Printed in the United States of America
ISBN 0-940931-17-6

Contents

Books by Gordon H. Clark

Readings in Ethics (1931)
Selections from Hellenistic Philosophy (1940)
A History of Philosophy (coauthor, 1941)
A Christian Philosophy of Education (1946)
A Christian View of Men and Things (1952)
What Presbyterians Believe (1956)[1]
Thales to Dewey (1957)
Dewey (1960)
Religion, Reason and Revelation (1961, 1986)
William James (1963)
Karl Barth's Theological Method (1963)
The Philosophy of Science and Belief in God (1964, 1987)
What Do Presbyterians Believe? (1965, 1985)
Peter Speaks Today (1967)[2]
The Philosophy of Gordon H. Clark (1968)
Biblical Predestination (1969)[3]
Historiography: Secular and Religious (1971)
II Peter (1972)[2]
The Johannine Logos (1972)
Three Types of Religious Philosophy (1973)
First Corinthians (1975)
Colossians (1979)
Predestination in the Old Testament (1979)[3]
I and II Peter (1980)
Language and Theology (1980)
First John (1980)
God's Hammer: The Bible and Its Critics (1982, 1987)
Behaviorism and Christianity (1982)
Faith and Saving Faith (1983)
In Defense of Theology (1984)
The Pastoral Epistles (1984)
The Biblical Doctrine of Man (1984)
The Trinity (1985)
Logic (1985)
Ephesians (1985)
Clark Speaks From the Grave (1986)
Logical Criticisms of Textual Criticism (1986)
First and Second Thessalonians (1986)
Predestination (1987)
The Atonement (1987)

[1] Revised in 1965 as *What Do Presbyterians Believe?*
[2] Combined in 1980 as *I & II Peter*.
[3] Combined in 1987 as *Predestination*.

Foreword

In these days of health care for all, education for all, rights for all, and opportunity for all, it seems almost inevitable that the Gospel of Jesus Christ would be obscured by the popular religious teaching of salvation for all. The democratic ideals of equality and equal opportunity have invaded theology as well as politics.

Most churches in the United States that call themselves Christian reject the Gospel. They teach, if they are liberal, that Jesus was a good man, even a martyr, but he died in no one's place; or, if they are conservative, that Jesus died in everyone's place, desires all men to be saved, and offers salvation to all. But it really makes little difference whether a church is large, respectable and liberal and teaches that Jesus died for no one; or enthusiastic, growing, and conservative and teaches that Jesus died for everyone: The result is the same: Jesus Christ actually saves no one—no one at all. Both liberals and conservatives agree that people save themselves by an exercise of their wills. The conservative "Christ" makes salvation possible, if people will only let him into their hearts; the liberal "Christ" points the way to salvation, if people will but follow his example. Neither "Christ" saves.

The liberals are perhaps more forthright in denying the Gospel; they say that Jesus was just a good example or a good teacher. They don't pretend to present a Saviour. The conservatives disguise the fact that they have no Gospel—no good news—by saying that God loves everyone and offers salvation to all. But the meaning of both the liberal message and the conservative message is the same: Neither a good moral teacher nor a mere offer of salvation actually saves. Neither the liberals nor the conservatives, the humanists nor the Arminians, have a Saviour. The liberal "Christ," at best, is a brave soul who endures injustice rather than renounce his belief in humankind; the conservative "Christ" is a wimp who begs people to let him into their hearts.

What neither liberals nor conservatives, Protestants nor Roman Catholics, charismatics nor fundamentalists will teach is the Biblical doctrine of the Atonement: God the Father, possessing all power and all knowledge, from eternity chose the specific individuals he would save; God the Son, possessing all power and all knowledge, became flesh in order to propitiate the wrath of the Father by dying in the place of those whom the Father had chosen; and God the Holy Spirit, possessing all power and all knowledge, irresistibly and in due time gives the persons elected by the Father and ransomed by the Son the faith and salvation that Christ earned for them. This Biblical doctrine of the Atonement is the Gospel, the good news, about what God has done for his people. It is the good news about Jesus Christ, the author and finisher of our faith. Salvation is a gift of God to his people from beginning to end.

Biblical theology, particularly the doctrine of the Atonement, is undemocratic; it clashes with the modern ideals of equality and equal opportunity. But God is not an equal opportunity Saviour. Christ died for and prays for only those whom the Father sent him to save. It is to them alone that the gift of faith will be given. It is them alone that Christ actually saves. Their salvation illustrates the mercy of God, for they have no claim on their Creator, and they are as sinful as those damned.

The damnation of the reprobate illustrates God's justice. Both the elect and the damned illustrate his sovereignty.

Many of those whom God has predestined to Hell have been very religious people. Two thousand years ago, they were the religious leaders of Israel, the Scribes and the Pharisees. Not much seems to have changed in the past two thousand years, for today many unbelievers attend, support, and lead large churches and religious organizations in the United States; they are described in Matthew 7:

> Not everyone who says to me, "Lord, Lord," shall enter the kingdom of heaven, but he who does the will of my Father in Heaven.
>
> Many will say to me in that day, "Lord, Lord, have we not prophesied in your name and cast out demons in your name, and done many wonders in your name?"
>
> And then I will declare to them, "I never knew you; depart from me, you who practice lawlessness!"

The doctrine of the Atonement is the heart of the Biblical message. It is this Christian doctrine, together with the doctrine of the inerrancy of Scripture, on which the world in its diabolical wisdom has concentrated its attacks. In this book Dr. Clark brings an unmatched clarity of thought and expression to a critical Christian doctrine, and his systematic explanation of the Atonement will richly reward the believing reader. But to those who are perishing, as Paul says, the message of this book will be the smell of death. We pray that the Eternal and Almighty God, who works all things according to his own will among the hosts of heaven and earth, will cause those who read *The Atonement* to believe the truth about our Lord and Saviour Jesus Christ.

John W. Robbins
December 12, 1986

Deuteronomy 6:6,7:	These words . . . shall be in thine heart, and thou shalt teach them diligently to thy children, and shalt talk of them . . . .
Deuteronomy 17:19:	He shall read therein all the days of his life . . . .
Psalm 1:2:	His delight is in the law of the Lord, and in his law doth he meditate day and night.
Psalm 119:97:	O how love I thy law, it is my meditation all the day.
Psalm 119:148:	My eyes prevent [precede] the [night] watches that I might meditate in thy word.
John 5:39:	Search the Scriptures . . . .
John 17:17:	Sanctify them through thy truth: thy word is truth.
Acts 17:11:	These . . . searched the Scriptures daily.
Colossians 3:16:	Let the word of Christ dwell in you richly in all wisdom.

These verses in one way or another stress the necessity of reading, understanding, and tracing out the implications of God's written revelation. Someone might wonder why II Timothy 2:15 was not quoted. Does it not command us to *study* the Scriptures? And does not the present writer wish to emphasize studying the Scriptures? Well, the Greek word is not *study*. But let not the intellectually lazy person rejoice. The Greek verb means *be eager, make every effort, be zealous* to arrive at a correct understanding of the word of truth.

This opening page has not exhibited, nor has it seemed to promise, any great degree of profound scholarship. But appearances are deceptive. The first step is to get the ordinary church members, who have unwittingly absorbed the anti-intellectual proclivities of neo-orthodoxy, to realize that God speaks the truth, and that he spoke the truth so that we might gain an understanding of his mind; so that also we ourselves might have the mind of Christ. Nowhere are we told to have the emotions of Christ. But Scripture repeats and repeats the exhortation to understand divine truth. This is God's command, though obedience to it is often quite difficult.

This treatise will soon become very complicated because the doctrine of the Atonement is very complicated, far more complicated than the vast majority of Christians can imagine. Learned theologians may look down their noses at quoting a few disjointed passages. The more erudite books assume that their readers already know these verses. Such an assumption was perhaps once justified, but hardly now. At any rate a few easy quotations may possibly entice an unsuspecting pew-warmer to dive into theology before he realizes the dangers of not being able to swim. But how can one learn to swim without jumping in? Other verses will be quoted later as they are needed; but these are an easy, perhaps deceptively easy, beginning.

Genesis 3:15:	It shall bruise thy head, and thou shall bruise his heel.
Isaiah 53:5,11:	He was wounded for our transgressions . . . he shall see of the travail of his soul and shall be satisfied.
Matthew 1:21:	Thou shalt call his name Jesus, for he shall save his people from their sins.
I Peter 2:24:	Who his own self bare our sins in his own body on the tree . . . by whose stripes ye were healed.

In addition to the information these verses provide, their

use bears on the distinction between exposition and apologetics, or at least some apologetics. Taking into consideration the entire Christian enterprise, should we limit ourselves to Scripture, and arguments based thereon, or should we find premises in sincere, common opinion, human experience, from which we can establish the basic principles of Christianity and so justify the use of revelation? Although a final conclusion on this point is inappropriate so early in the discussion, the reader must not be left unaware of its pervasive importance. One example, to be discussed more fully later on, may be introduced by another scriptural quotation. In a tremendous paragraph Paul wrote,

Romans 3:26: . . . that he might be just and the justifier of him which believeth in Jesus.

This verse says something about the *justice* of God, and the justice of God is a most important facet of doctrine of the Atonement. But at the moment we are interested only in the *method* used to defend divine justice. Here is an example.

Jonathan Edwards wrote a thirty-five page article *Concerning the Necessity and Reasonableness of the Christian Doctrine of Satisfaction for Sin* (*Works*, Vol. VIII, 1811). He introduces his subject with the proposition that "Justice requires that sin be punished." He appeals to the universal belief that "some crimes are so horrid . . . that it is requisite they should not go unpunished unless . . . some measure [of compensation or repentance] at least balances the desert of punishment. . . ." In Jonathan Edwards' day hardly anyone would have disagreed, and thus Edwards could rely on the commonly held view as a sufficient introduction to his theology. Today that is not the case. Many people hold that crime is only a disease, the criminal is not guilty, but sick, and even his sickness is the result of a misguided society rather than of a depraved individual mind or will. If then it be our business to maintain the truth of the Christian doctrine of Atonement, instead of merely explaining it, we must face a problem Edwards hardly dreamed of. In view of the prevalent behaviorism and Freudian psychology, we cannot rely on common opinion and so-called human reason. Yet if we depend on revelation alone, are we not begging the question and losing our audience? Edwards could plausibly appeal to human reason because the human reason he was acquainted with was English reason already permeated with Christian ideas. But this is no longer the case. Edwards thought that crime excites "such an abhorrence and indignation that . . . by this all is granted that needs to be granted, to show that desert of punishment carries in it a requisiteness of the punishment deserved" (p. 500). But today the behaviorists (*e.g.* John Watson and B.F. Skinner) aim to remove the idea of punishment from the laws and from the mind of man. Sweden, for example, has made it illegal for parents to spank their children or even to scold them. Naturally: Socialism is anti-Christian.

From the eighteenth century Christian opinion that all crime demands punishment, unless there be something to balance it, Edwards infers that, since any sin against God is so great that nothing can balance it, God must punish it. "If any ask, why God could not pardon the injury on repentance, without other satisfaction, without wrong to justice; I ask the same person why he could not also pardon the injury *without* repentance?" To Edwards this is unthinkable; but few today would acknowledge that his argument is valid. On the next page (p. 502) he appeals not only to a Christian conscience, but also to "the consciences of heathen." Yet he must add the damaging proviso "unless conscience has been stupified by frequent violations." On page 506 he also admits "all but

Epicureans will own that all moral agents are subjects of God's moral government." This is a false statement. Others than Epicureans are also such exceptions. Of course Jonathan Edwards antedated the modern Logical Positivists, who are far from being Epicureans, but in addition to Democritus, not even Aristotle satisfies Edwards' assertion. For that matter, even one exception to his norm destroys his position. Yet from his inadequate observation he concludes that therefore God's conscience must be like ours. Hence Edwards' argument fails on two counts: invalid inference and false premises.

To conclude this first section and to anticipate, the method used here will be first, some exposition, plus here and there the drawing of inferences from the verses quoted; then, second, the refutation of two sorts of arguments–well-meaning but inadequate defenses of the Biblical truths and definite attacks on the Christian faith.

2. The Doctrine in Its Simplicity

An individual Christian, without scholarly ambitions, reads the Bible and notes certain statements concerning the death of Christ. With further meditation, if he qualifies as an example of Psalm 1:2, he will realize that several verses say pretty much the same thing, while another half dozen make a different point. This procedure will in time result in an elementary understanding of the Atonement divided into four or five or six points. These points could be that Christ's death was (1) a sacrifice, for I Corinthians 5:7 says, "Christ our Passover is sacrificed for us;" (2) an expiatory sacrifice, for Matthew 26:28 speaks of "my blood . . . which is shed for many for the remission of sins;" (3) a vicarious or substitutionary sacrifice, for Mark 10:45 says that "the Son of Man came . . . to give his life a ransom for many;" (4) a propitiation, for II

Corinthians 5:18 says "God has reconciled us to himself through Christ;" and (5) a satisfaction of divine justice, for Romans 3:25, 26 specifies both propitiation and satisfaction: "whom God hath set forth to be a propitiation . . . that he might be just and the justifier of him which believeth in Jesus."

After further study, indeed after much further study and discussion among themselves, groups of devout men tried to summarize the Biblical teaching. Their statements may not have reproduced every jot and tittle of the teaching, but some formulations were remarkably complete. There were at times individual authors who wrote books on the subject, of whom Anselm is one of the best known; but the reference here is to groups of theologians who wrote short summaries, at least shorter than a book. The best and most important of these summaries—and this is not just my opinion alone—is chapter eight of the Westminster Confession. This document is more than a summary of the doctrine of the Atonement. From 1643 to 1649 (theoretically until 1652) approximately sixty to seventy of the most learned English and Scottish theologians worked on a summary of all the main Biblical teachings. No document since that date comes anywhere near superseding it. Chapter eight will now be quoted, but first, in view of some contemporary confusion, a distinction should be made.

In 1924 a document called the Auburn Affirmation was signed and published by some 1300 ministers of the Presbyterian Church in the U.S.A. These 1300 ministers unanimously rejected the inerrancy of Scripture, and in addition asserted that the doctrines of the Virgin Birth, the miracles, the Atonement, and the Resurrection are unessential. They somewhat disguised their unbelief by stating that they all believed in the *fact* of the Atonement, though which *doctrine* of the Atonement to accept was unimportant. This attempt to distinguish between the fact of the Atonement and the doctrine of the Atonement is obfuscating. The Atonement is a doctrine, not a fact. The Old Testament, and to a lesser extent the New Testament as well, contain many statements of historical events: the flood, Abraham's migration to Palestine, the Exodus, and the fact that David was born into the tribe of Judah. So what? Other people migrated and other children were born into the tribe of Judah and still others into the tribe of Ephraim. So what? Jesus' death was also an historical event. It took place on Friday, the fourteenth of Nisan in the year A.D. 30 (or thereabouts). But the death of two thieves at the same time and place was also an historical event. Eventually Pontius Pilate died, and so too the High Priest. The death of Jesus as a bare historical event would be as unimportant as theirs. The tremendous difference between Jesus' death and the deaths of the others is its significance. The Bible recounts the event, to be sure, but it also adds the explanation of the event. The doctrine of the Atonement is that explanation. This doctrine or explanation is no temporal occurrence: It is a part of the divine plan, an eternal thought in the mind of God. What God's eternal thought is, he revealed in the Bible; and the Westminster Confession summarizes the Biblical teaching. The five points mentioned in the first paragraph of this subsection give the simplest Biblical form; other verses should be added to them by each person who reads the Bible; the Westminster Confession aims to summarize these verses. Its summary is not quite so simple as the verses. But it is not beyond the grasp of an average intellect.

It pleased God, in his eternal purpose, to choose and ordain the Lord Jesus, his only-begotten Son, to be the Mediator between God and man; the Prophet, Priest, and King; the Head and Saviour of his Church; the Heir of all things; and Judge of the world; unto whom he did, from all eternity, give a people to be his seed, and to be by him in time redeemed, called, justified, sanctified, and glorified.[1]

Some editions of the Confession print out eight or ten verses in support of the text; other editions give only book, chapter and verse. For example, in section one, the eternal purpose of God to choose Jesus Christ as mediator is supported by Isaiah 42:1, "Behold my servant, whom I uphold; *mine elect*, in whom my soul delighteth. *I have put my Spirit upon him*; he shall bring forth judgment to the Gentiles." There follow four other verses to the same purpose. As one familiar with the Scriptures may suppose, these are not the only verses which shed light on the Father's eternal choice of Christ. They are samples only. The footnote to the final phrase of VIII, viii gives six verses. First year seminary students and every Bible-loving Christian should familiarize himself with such material.

It will be of historical interest as well as of theological importance to quote a bit of the Confession of the Waldenses. It was written somewhat as an appeal to the Protestant nations in consequence of a frightful and barbarous massacre of the Waldenses by the Romanists. Cromwell in England out of his own pocket donated 2000 pounds and thus initiated a public subscription for the alleviation of the survivors. Some £38,000 were raised; but as Cromwell died about then, the licentious and semi-catholic Charles II purloined about £16,000. Here is a part of the Confession: "We believe . . . that God saves from this corruption and condemnation those whom he has chosen of his mercy in Jesus Christ his Son; passing by all the rest, according to the irreprehensible reason of his freedom and justice."

Some fifty years before these two creeds the English

---

1. Chapter VIII, section 1.

church had adopted its Thirty-nine Articles, of which the XXXI is as follows:

> The offering of Christ once made is that perfect redemption, propitiation, and satisfaction, for all the sins of the whole world, both original and actual; and there is none other satisfaction for sin but that alone. Wherefore the sacrifices of Masses, in which it was commonly said that the Priest did offer Christ for the quick and the dead, to have remission of pain and guilt, were blasphemous fables and dangerous deceits.

These then are simple but official statements of the doctrine this treatise aims to examine.

3. The Covenant of Redemption

The simplicity of the passion narratives in the four Gospels begins to become complex for us when we realize that the events have an eternal significance. The doctrine of the Atonement is a part, a most important part, of the divine and omniscient plan of the universe. It is not a temporal event: It is an eternal decree. The extremely puzzling relationship between time and eternity is the worst complexity embedded in the doctrine of the Atonement, and in all Biblical doctrines, for all are related to and dependent on the eternal God. Such a difficulty is hardly appropriate for any elementary study of the Bible; yet it cannot be totally avoided. Perhaps it will be pedagogically but not theoretically sufficient to pin-point the difficulty and press on.

As with every problem, the most important step is to define the terms. Augustine of Hippo made the frequently quoted remark, If you do not ask me what time is, I know, but if you ask me, I do not know. Sir Isaac Newton posited time and space as the two independent frameworks within which everything happens. But today apparently no scientist accepts this view. A decrease in velocity increases the diameter of an object—or something like that. *The Encyclopedia of Philosophy*, edited by Paul Edwards, has several articles on "Time." Most readers will find them unintelligible. Secular scientists are not interested in eternity, but secular philosophers, even pagan philosophers like Plato, are.

It is pedagogically unsound to follow this subject very far in this treatise. Yet a hint may be of some help. Augustine, for all his hesitation, defined time as the sequence of ideas in a created mind. Perhaps this is circular and begs the question; but on this ground we may define eternity as omniscience. There is no sequence of ideas in God's mind: no temporal sequence. If there were, God would know some things today he did not know yesterday. But omniscience means that God always knows everything. Ideas do not come and go. His mind, that is, God himself, is immutable; he is not subject to change. Hence we talk of an eternal decree. God's plan of the universe never began and was never altered. This includes the doctrine of the Atonement, as the Confession says, "It pleased God, in his eternal purpose, to choose and ordain the Lord Jesus . . . ."

This choice can and has been called the Covenant of Redemption.

No matter how ill-prepared a young Christian student may be, he can hardly be ignorant of the fact that the Bible prescribes a method by which sinners are to be forgiven, escape the penalty for sin, and find favor with God. Biblical theologians have often divided the preparatory steps to this actual salvation into two covenants: the covenant of redemption and the covenant of grace. This is a convenient division because, even if some theologians want to merge them and use only the second title, there are two stages in the preparation for the Atonement and its application, and these two must both be included

somewhere in the discussion. The division depends on the first①
part's being a relation between the Father and the Son, while the
second part is a relation between the Son and the people he ②
came to save. What is worse than merging these two parts is the
outright denial of the first part by several non-Calvinistic
theologians. Their reasons for such a denial are two. First, the
general theology of Arminianism prevents the acknowledgment of the covenant of redemption. To answer this objection
one must show that Augustine, Calvin and Hodge correctly
understood the Bible, whereas Arminius did not. The second
reason for not acknowledging the covenant of redemption is the
impression that the Bible nowhere describes such a consultation
between the Father and the Son. This narrower and more direct
objection can be answered by showing that such an agreement
between the Father and the Son is by no means an obscure idea
buried in one or two subsidiary phrases. On the contrary, the
Scripture gives a quite ample foundation to the doctrine. To
show that there is indeed a covenant of redemption, a dozen
verses will first be quoted and then exegesis will follow.

Luke 22:29:	And I assign to you, as my Father assigned to me, a kingdom.
John 5:30:	I cannot on my own authority do anything; as I hear, I judge, and my judgment is just because I seek not my own will, but the will of the Father who sent me.
John 5:43:	I am come in my Father's name.
John 6:37-39:	Everything that the Father gives to me will come to me, and him who comes to me, I shall not cast out; because I descended from heaven not to do my own will, but the will of him who sent me. And this is the will of

him who sent me: that I should lose nothing of what he gave me, but that I should raise it on the last day.

John 8:42:
I proceeded forth and came from God; neither came I of myself, but he sent me.

John 10:29:
My Father, who gave them to me, is greater than all.

John 17:6ff:
. . . the men that thou gavest me out of the world; thine they were, and thou gavest them to me . . . for I have given them the words thou gavest me . . . those whom thou hast given me, etc.

Romans 5:19:
. . . by the obedience of one [i.e., of Jesus to his Father.]

Romans 8:3:
God sending his own Son . . . .

Ephesians 1:4-5:
. . . he hath chosen us in him . . . having predestinated us . . . by Jesus Christ.

Ephesians 3:11:
. . . the eternal purpose which he purposed in Christ Jesus our Lord.

II Timothy 1:9:
. . . according to his own purpose and grace, which was given us in Christ Jesus before the world began.

This list of verses is longer than usual because some theologians deny the concept and some pastors think that if there be such a covenant it is too unimportant to preach about. A study of the Scripture, an exegesis of these verses, should dispel the objections.

The first of these verses quoted states that the Father assigned a task to the Son. The verb *assign* means to make a will or covenant. It has the same root as the New *Testament* has. The Father is here described as making a will, a testament, or a covenant with the Son. The Son clearly accepted the assignment, for in fulfillment of the task the Father gave him, he gives a similar assignment to his disciples.

The next two verses teach that the Son does not act on his individual authority alone: He is intent on accomplishing his Father's will—he acts in his Father's name. Obviously there must have been some agreement between the Father and the Son before the Son's incarnation. John 8:42 repeats these ideas.

John 6:37-39 not only repeats that the Son does the Father's will, but in addition specifies what this will is. With John 10 and John 17 they all teach that the Father selected a certain group of people out of the world as the particular persons whom the Son was to save. This is not said just once, but is repeated several times in this group of verses.

The context of Romans 5:19 expounds a comparison between Adam and Christ. Since the disobedience of the first Adam reflects a covenant of works with God, the comparison naturally suggests some sort of covenant between the Father and the Son. Otherwise the comparison would be completely adventitious and inconsistent with an omniscient plan of redemption. The same may be said of the extremely condensed statement in I Corinthians 15:21-22.

Romans 8:3 may not add much, but at least it repeats the same idea: God sent his Son to do a certain task. All these verses indicate a divine plan to save certain people by Jesus Christ. This predestination occurred according to the good pleasure of God's will. The relation of the Father to the Son is twice made explicit, though not emphasized, in Ephesians 1:4-5. Greater emphasis comes in Ephesians 3:11 because the verse is shorter than the preceding, with its several additional phrases omitted. Because of these omissions the idea of the eternal purpose which the Father purposed in Christ Jesus our Lord receives the

exclusive emphasis. II Timothy 1:9 clearly indicates that the
elect received grace by Christ before the world began. Obviously Christ agreed to carry out this plan in time. Lest the list be
thought too long, be it noted that I Peter 1:2 also indicates a
concerted plan in which the three persons of the Trinity all have
a part.

As a concluding Scriptural emphasis, another pertinent
verse is

Hebrews 10:7:   Lo, I come ... to do thy will, O
                                     God.

This verse clearly requires an agreement by the Son to
fulfill what the Father willed him to do. Does not this justify a
theologian's acceptance of the concept of a Covenant of
Redemption?

The main terms of the Covenant are set forth in the several
passages quoted. Some specifications and developments can be
more appropriately discussed under later sub-heads; but the
chief idea is that the Son consented to atone for the sins of those
people whom the Father had given to him. The method of this
development is of course the full doctrine: his incarnation, his
death, his satisfaction of divine justice, and, if one wish, his
resurrection with its consequences. Since all these things lead
into or are a part of the Covenant of Grace, it is well to note that
for Christ himself the Covenant of Redemption was not a
Covenant of Grace. The two covenants, admittedly both parts
of a unitary eternal decree, are essentially distinct because for
Christ the Covenant of Redemption was a covenant of works. It
was necessary for him to live a sinless life, in full obedience to
the Law, and then to bear the penalty due to the sinners he came
to save. Christ *earned* salvation.

For sermonic material many verses invite some reference

to this covenant. Hebrews 10:5 indicates that the Father prepared a suitable body for the Son's incarnation. Isaiah 42:1-7 recounts certain promises the Father made to the Son. Acts 2:27 quotes the promise of Psalm 16:10 as the context describes its fulfillment.

It is clear, therefore, that the Covenant of Redemption is not an invention of imaginative theologians; nor is it an obscure implication buried in a few brief phrases; on the contrary, all these verses teach (1) that the Son came to earth on the authority of the Father who sent him; (2) that the Father had given him a definite number of people to save; and (3) several other things that will be pertinent later. But the first two points, which could be deduced from the doctrine of omniscience plus the historical events, are clearly made explicit. And this is equivalent to the assertion that an agreement or covenant between the Father and the Son existed from all eternity.

4. The Covenant of Grace

Although the word *covenant* has been constantly used in the preceding discussion, it may be wise, before the details of the Covenant of Grace are taken up, to say a little more about the idea or definition of a covenant. This is particularly appropriate because the Presbyterian and Reformed denominations have historically taught "Covenant Theology." That is to say, these churches have viewed the Scripture as a developing revelation—developing from a less detailed to a more detailed form—of a single plan of salvation. This single theme, the Bible calls a covenant; and by this covenant between God and his people, the latter are prepared for and are brought to its complete fruition in heaven.

The preceding section assumed that a covenant was an agreement between two or more persons. Although this is the standard Calvinistic definition, sometimes it is said to be incorrect. It does indeed run the risk of producing a misunderstanding. In these days agreements or contracts are usually drawn up by two or more fairly equal parties. At least, even the weakest party might force acceptance of one or two subordinate clauses. In the Covenant of Grace, however, sinful man has no say as to what the terms of the covenant shall be. Therefore the transaction might be called an imposition, a promise, a command, but hardly a contract. While such a misunderstanding is possible, yet it is not an objection to defining covenant as an agreement. The most frequently repeated covenant in the Old Testament was the marriage covenant. Yet in those times the wife was not the equal of the husband, nor for that matter did the groom have full liberty in setting the terms of the agreement. Neither does a Christian couple today have the authority to formulate the main terms. The idea of *agreement* therefore requires neither that the parties be equal, nor that the parties themselves determine the conditions. Yet when they accept the conditions, an agreement exists.

The terms of the Covenant of Grace are indeed dictated by God. No man can change them. The Covenant is wholly divine in its origin and specifications. In fact so true is this that God says, "I will establish my covenant with thee." He does not ask, Shall we formulate a covenant? Noah agreed, and the account of Noah's relation to God will serve as a good example.

Without denying the idea of agreement, it is worthwhile to emphasize the divine initiative. Not just once, but at least four times in the account of Noah, God says, "I establish my covenant with you." In addition to these four assertions, God also said, "I do set my bow in the cloud," and "I will remember my covenant." The rainbow is not so much to remind Noah of God's covenant, as to remind God himself: "the bow shall be seen in the cloud, and I will remember. . . . I will look upon it that I may remember the everlasting covenant" (Genesis 9:8-17).

The terms of the covenant with Noah have to do with the divine promise not to destroy the earth by flood again. The text does not explicitly mention salvation from sin. Yet, since the flood came because of the great sinfulness of the race, and since Noah was saved from the immediate punishment of this sin, the whole may be taken as a type or anticipation of a still greater salvation. Therefore the covenant with Noah may properly be viewed as an early form of the Covenant of Grace. God explained the covenant in fuller detail to Abraham, and these details Moses, by inspiration, recorded.

In Abraham's case the divine initiative is even clearer than it was with Noah, if that were possible. Genesis 15:18 says, "In the same day the Lord made a covenant with Abram . . . ." Note: It does not say that the Lord and Abram made a covenant between themselves, but "the Lord made a covenant with Abram." Not only are there explicit assertions in Genesis 15:18 and 17:2, 7, plus other verses in the latter chapter, but there is also in the previous chapter the awesome horror of great darkness in which Abram was a totally passive recipient of prophecy. Moses also in Exodus 24:8 expresses the divine initiative. David also, in II Samuel 23:5. Then Isaiah 55:3 reads, "I will make an everlasting covenant with you, even the sure mercies of David." Compare Jeremiah 31:31-33. The definition of a covenant as an agreement is intended to cover both God's covenants, the marriage covenant, and other contracts. If, however, the word *agreement* obscures the idea that God sovereignly imposes the terms, then perhaps it may be thought wise to drop the word agreement and use some other word. Yet, this would be unfortunate, for Abraham surely agreed to the terms.

The terms of the Covenant of Grace are no more than

slightly hinted at in Genesis 3:15. A bit more explicit is God's revelation to Abraham in Genesis 13, where God promises to bless Abraham and in him all the families of the earth, though he will curse those who curse Abraham. Greater detail comes in the horror of great darkness in Genesis 15; and other details, including circumcision as a sign of the covenant, in Genesis 17. The extent of the covenant is not merely limited to the descendants of Abraham, but "in Isaac shall thy seed be called." It is not necessary, however, to trace the historical development of the revelation through the Old Testament, for as the whole is the doctrine of the Atonement, its details will be covered in the systematic exposition.

A few paragraphs above there was a reference to the "Covenant Theology" of the Presbyterian and Reformed churches. Though the aim here is to show that this theology is Biblical, as are the doctrines of the Trinity and the two natures of Christ, yet in the history of Christendom none of these three doctrines was well understood for centuries after the apostles. Perhaps the credit of having discovered this doctrine may be assigned to Zwingli. Calvin mentions the doctrine, but his emphasis is on other matters. Ursinus in Germany and a bit later Ussher in Ireland developed the idea. The Westminster Assembly gave it confessional status. In Holland Cocceius popularized it—though he unfortunately added a few fanciful details. The Anabaptists denied the Covenant of Grace, as did some Baptists before John Gill; and naturally the Arminians, Wesleyans, and Methodists found no place for it. Its frequent mention in the Scripture, however, makes such denials or neglect a strange phenomenon among those who profess to accept the Bible.

More recently the opposite extreme of multiplying covenants or dispensations has given rise to Dispensationalism. The Scofield Bible enumerates seven dispensations. It defines *dispensation* in the sub-head to Genesis 1:28: "A dispensation is a period of time during which man is tested in respect of obedience to some *specific* revelation of the will of God." In itself this definition is not particularly bad. Old Testament history describes several occasions when God tested man by some *specific* revelation. This was true not only of Noah, Abraham, and Moses, but also of many others. There are several cases in Judges, such as the testing of Gideon by reducing his army as described in the seventh chapter. Then there is the case of Saul and Agag (I Samuel 15:3, 8, 14); Saul failed the test, Gideon passed the test. Then too there is the case of David's numbering the people (II Samuel 24:1, 10, 12). These, however, are not what Scofield means by dispensations, even though they are cases of God's testing men by a special revelation. Scofield enumerates seven dispensations. Even this, though somewhat fanciful, is nothing to cause great alarm. The description of the first dispensation in the footnote to Genesis 1:28 is quite good. The really serious error, the actually fatal error, of dispensationalism is the construing of these dispensations so as to provide, since the fall, two (or more) separate and distinct plans of salvation. Lewis Sperry Chafer wrote, "There are two widely different, standardized, divine provisions, whereby man, who is utterly fallen may come into the favor of God" (*Bibliotheca Sacra*, Vol. 93, 1936, p. 410). On I John 3:7, "he that doeth righteousness is righteous," the Scofield Bible's note is in part, ". . . The righteous man under law became righteous by doing righteously; under grace he does righteously because he has been made righteous." Thus instead of a covenant of grace, extending from Adam, through Abraham, into Galatians, and on to the culmination, dispensationalism has two methods of salvation.

For example, Scofield's footnote to Romans 7:6 speaks of "two methods of divine dealing: one through the law, the other

through the Holy Spirit." Now, Paul before his conversion may
have had a wrong conception of the Mosaic law, but this does
not mean that in reality the Holy Spirit was inoperative in the
Old Testament. Similarly the footnote to John 1:17, "Grace . . .
is constantly set in contrast to law, under which God demands
righteousness from man . . . ." But God still demands righteousness from man, though this righteousness is a gift from God.
The righteousness by which an Old Testament saint was saved
was also a divine gift. Therefore Scofield is quite wrong in the
following footnote, which says, "As a dispensation grace begins
with the death and resurrection of Christ. . . . The point of
testing is no longer legal obedience as the condition of salvation
. . . ." But the dispensation of grace did not begin with the
crucifixion. God began dispensing grace to Adam. Furthermore, legal obedience was not the condition of salvation in the
Mosaic "dispensation." The condition was faith in a future
sacrifice.

This radical deviation from the doctrine that salvation in
all ages can be found in Christ alone results in another amazing
distortion of the Old Testament. In his note on Matthew 4:17
Scofield says, and to insure against the charge of misrepresentation by omission the note will be reproduced in its entirety,
viz.,

> "At hand" is never a positive affirmation that the person or thing
> said to be "at hand" will immediately appear, but only that no
> known or predicted event must intervene. When Christ ap-
> peared to the Jewish people, the next thing, in the order of
> revelation as it then stood, should have been the setting up of the
> Davidic kingdom. In the knowledge of God, not yet disclosed,
> lay the rejection of the kingdom (and King), the long period of
> the mystery-form of the kingdom, the world-wide preaching of
> the cross, and the out-calling of the Church. But this was as yet

locked up in the secret counsels of God (Mt. 13.11, 17; Eph. 3.3-10).

This footnote should be carefully examined to see how fatally heretical it is. Whether "at hand" actually means what Scofield says is unimportant. What is important is that Scofield takes it to mean that "no known or predicted event must intervene" before what is "at hand." Hence when Jesus says that the Kingdom is at hand, Scofield concludes that the Old Testament has no prediction of anything that occurs between the moment of Jesus' preaching and his second advent to institute the millennium. This means that the Old Testament contains no prophecy concerning the Atonement. Incredible as this is for an interpretation of the Old Testament, Scofield puts this quite explicitly: "When Christ appeared to the Jewish people, the next thing in the order of revelation as it then stood [*i.e.*, in the Old Testament prophecies] should have been the setting up of the Davidic Kingdom. In the knowledge of God, not yet disclosed [*i.e.*, not prophesied in the Old Testament] lay the rejection of the kingdom (and King) [Scofield's parenthesis includes the crucifixion and resurrection]. . . . This was as yet locked up in the secret counsels of God." This is an explicit denial that there is any prophecy in the Old Testament relating to the crucifixion. "The world-wide preaching of the cross" including the events of Pentecost, which Peter said was the fulfillment of a prophecy by Joel, was all locked up in God's secret counsel. Incredible!

Though it may not be spelled out so explicitly, the footnote to Matthew 5:2 in effect says that sinners during the millennium will be saved, not by the blood, merits, and grace of Christ, but by their obedience to the beatitudes, which are "pure law."

But this contradicts the universal proposition of Acts 4:12: "Neither is there salvation in any other: for there is none other name under heaven given among men, whereby we must be saved."

The Scripture, quite the reverse of Dispensationalism, asserts that there is just one way of salvation. True enough, the divine plan in all its completeness, as Paul said in Ephesians 3:5, ". . . was not made known unto the sons of men in other ages as it is now revealed to his apostles and prophets by the Spirit;" but Paul's fuller doctrinal explanation is precisely the same covenant that was less fully revealed in Genesis 3:15: "I will put enmity between thee and the woman, and between thy seed and her seed; it shall bruise thy head, and thou shalt bruise his heel."

Though this is the fatal error that removes Dispensationalism from the sphere of evangelical Christianity, there are also some minor infelicities, which, though overshadowed, need not be overlooked.

When it comes to Noah, the Scofield Bible professes to see only a covenant of civil government. Supposedly this divine test of man is limited to civil government. If it has any bearing on salvation, it would seem that heaven is to be achieved through governmental agencies. If it has no bearing on eternal life, the theory faces two difficulties. The first and more important point is that the whole transaction must envisage salvation from sin. This background is the wickedness of the human race as described in Genesis 6. God decided to destroy mankind because of its sins; but

Genesis 6:8:   Noah found grace in the eyes of the
                     Lord.

Here then is the Covenant of Grace. Noah was not to be punished and destroyed with the others because

Genesis 6:18:   With thee will I establish my covenant.

Naturally the immediate deliverance is from the flood; but as the flood was the punishment for sin, it is hard to exclude an anticipation of a final and complete deliverance. Explicitly in the following chapter, it says

Genesis 7:1:   Thee have I seen righteous before me.

The underlying motif therefore is sin and salvation, not merely a flood and escape from drowning. But if this be the case, one cannot suppose that Noah achieved heaven on the ground that he instituted civil government.

In the second place, it is hard to find any reference to civil government at all. Chapter nine does indeed mention capital punishment; but this can be inflicted, and was inflicted, by the family of the murdered man. This supposition is strengthened by the word "brother" in Genesis 9:5. Civil government simply does not appear. Instead, if anyone wishes to exclude salvation from sin, the passage becomes simply a covenant or promise not to cause another world-wide flood. But though this is the immediate concern, such an interpretation discounts the cause and purpose of the flood.

It is on the Abrahamic covenant that Dispensationalism most obviously founders. A supposed antithesis between the Abrahamic covenant and the Mosaic dispensation, plus the antithesis and mutual incompatibility between both and the New Testament Covenant of Grace is a contradiction of both Testaments. Even in the so-called Mosaic dispensation, Deuteronomy 1:9 and 4:31, briefly and partially, yet unmistakably, appeal to the covenant with Abraham. In an earlier passage Moses prays for forgiveness on the basis of the promise to Abraham (Exodus 32:13). More clearly, Leviticus 26:42 specifies the Abrahamic covenant as the basis for God's dealing with the Israelites after the Exodus. The unity of the covenant and its application during the time of David is expressed in

Psalm 105:8-10:   He hath remembered his covenant
                                   for ever, the word which he com-
                                   manded to a thousand generations.
                                   Which covenant he made with Abra-
                                   ham, and his oath unto Isaac; and
                                   confirmed the same unto Jacob for a
                                   law, and to Israel for an everlasting
                                   covenant.

Note that it is an everlasting covenant, one that did not cease at
the Exodus.

But of course the clearest and most important passage is

Galatians 3:6-9,17:   Even as Abraham believed God,
                                   and it was accounted to him for
                                   righteousness. Know ye therefore that
                                   they which are of faith, the same are
                                   the children of Abraham. And the
                                   scripture, foreseeing that God would
                                   justify the heathen through faith,
                                   preached before the gospel unto
                                   Abraham, saying, In thee shall all
                                   nations be blessed. So then they which
                                   be of faith are blessed with faithful
                                   Abraham. And this I say, that the
                                   covenant, that was confirmed before
                                   of God in Christ, the law, which was
                                   four hundred and thirty years after,
                                   cannot disannul, that it should make
                                   the promise of none effect.

The first few verses of this quotation show that the elect in
New Testament times are saved on the basis of the Abrahamic

covenant and are counted as children of the patriarch. Further, these verses state that God's declaration to Abraham was in essence the very gospel that Paul preached. Not only so, but at the time of Abraham God explained to him that the covenant included the Gentiles. In the next place, Paul expressly affirms that the Mosaic "dispensation" could not disannul the Abrahamic covenant that four hundred and thirty years earlier had been confirmed in Christ. *In Christ*, no less. The Mosaic ritual, Paul explains, was a temporary arrangement necessary because of the sins of the Israelites. It was to cease when the Messiah should come. Even during the Mosaic administration, the Abrahamic covenant was not disannulled, set aside, invalidated, or made of no effect. The Abrahamic covenant was operative all through the alleged dispensation of law. No one was ever saved by keeping the law. No one ever kept the law. Salvation, now, then, and always has been by grace through faith. Hence from the fall of Adam there has been one, just one, continuing Covenant of Grace.

This unmasks another subsidiary though important instance in Scofield's footnote to Matthew 16:18: ". . . Israel was a true 'church,' but not in any sense the N.T. church—the only point of similarity being that both were 'called out' [*ek-klēsia*] and by the same God. All else is contrast."

But not all else is contrast. Israel and the New Testament Gentiles were not only as a matter of fact called out by the same God, they were called out to the same salvation from sin. This salvation in both cases depended on faith in the same promises. To say otherwise, as Scofield does, is to imply that either David or Cornelius failed to arrive in heaven.

Louis Berkhof (*Systematic Theology*, Eerdmans, 1939, [1968], p. 279), just before disposing of the dispensationalists in four lines, contrasts the Reformed doctrine with some earlier views. He writes:

It [the Covenant of Grace] is essentially the same in all dispensations, though its form of administration changes. This is contradicted by all those who claim that Old Testament saints were saved in another manner than New Testament believers, as for instance, Pelagians and Socinians, who hold that God gave additional help in the example and teachings of Christ; the Roman Catholics, who maintain that the Old Testament saints were in the *Limbus Patrum* until Christ's descent into hades; the followers of Coccejus, who assert that Old Testament believers enjoyed only a *paresis* (a passing over) and no *aphesis* (full forgiveness of sins); . . .

As hinted at a few paragraphs back, there are many facets of the doctrine of the Covenant of Grace that could be included here: the parties to the covenant; its nature, terms, and conditions; its aims and benefits; its administration both with the individual and in the corporate activity of the church. But these topics can be more logically put later.

5.   The Incarnation

By the term *incarnation*, a word of Latin derivation that could be crudely expressed as *enfleshment*, Christianity assumes that there was a person who existed before he was born. His birth, or conception, was the occasion of his appearing in flesh.

John 8:58:   Before Abraham was, I am.

Apart from the more profound significance of the words "I am," Jesus says at least that his existence did not commence in Bethlehem, but that it antedates Abraham. Hence the birth of Jesus was the birth of a preexistent person. That Jesus was preexistent does not of itself prove that he was God. Arius held that Jesus was a created angel, created before Abraham lived, but nonetheless a creature and not God. It is useless therefore to cite verses that say nothing more than Jesus existed before his birth. If Jesus was God, if the doctrine of the Trinity is true, preexistence cannot be denied.

Hence the importance of the last verse quoted does not lie in the words "Before Abraham was," but in the more profound concept of eternity embedded in the "I am" that recalls the words in Exodus. Thus the doctrine of the Incarnation overlaps the doctrine of the Deity of Christ and depends on the doctrine of the Trinity. Some Scripture references are now added.

> Matthew 16:16,17:   And Simon Peter answered and said, Thou art the Christ, the Son of the living God. And Jesus answered and said unto him, Blessed art thou, Simon Bar-jona: for flesh and blood hath not revealed it unto thee, but my Father which is in heaven.

Note here not only that Peter asserts Christ's Deity; and not only that Jesus accepts Peter's confession and indeed calls it a direct revelation from the Father; but note also that Matthew as the author records the event, and this recording is inspired–the words God breathed out onto the manuscript.

There is another form of phraseology that supports Jesus' preexistence and Deity. Matthew 22:44 with its parallels and Acts 2:34, 35 quote

> Psalm 110:1:   The LORD said unto my Lord, Sit thou at my right hand, until I make thine enemies thy footstool.

Many other verses refer to Jesus as Lord. They are too

numerous to list and too well known; but two will be given
nonetheless.

| Romans 10:9: | If thou shalt confess with thy mouth that Jesus is Lord . . . . |
| II Corinthians 13:14: | The grace of the Lord Jesus Christ . . . . |

About two centuries before the birth of Jesus the rabbis in
Alexandria, where the large Jewish population had largely
forgotten Hebrew, translated the Old Testament into Greek.
This translation, called the Septuagint, uses the Greek word
Kurios for the Hebrew *JHVH*. The New Testament, which
frequently uses the Septuagint translation, applies this Greek
title to Jesus: the Lord Jesus. Thus the authors of the New
Testament books identify Jesus as Jehovah.

For example Matthew 3:3 quotes Isaiah 40:3, "the way of
Jehovah" (compare Mark 1:3, Luke 3:4, and John 1:23). I
Corinthians 1:31 quotes Jeremiah 9:24, "Let him that glorieth
. . . understand . . . that I am Jehovah." Isaiah 8:13, "Sanctify
Jehovah" is repeated in I Peter 3:15 as "Sanctify Christ as
Lord."

Since these verses help to establish the doctrine of the
Trinity, and thus emphasize the Deity of Christ, the preexistence of the person born to Mary is also sufficiently established.
More particularly with reference to the event of incarnation
Louis Berkhof, perhaps bearing in mind the Eastern phrase
"God became man so that man might become God," (*Systematic Theology*, 4th ed., p. 333) writes, "It was not the triune God
but the second person of the Trinity that assumed human
nature. For that reason it is better to say that the Word became
flesh than that God became man. At the same time we should
remember that each of the divine persons was active in the

incarnation."

Berkhof then refers to:

Matthew 1:20:   Do not fear to take your wife Mary, for what is begotten in her is from the Holy Spirit. (Compare Luke 1:35.)

Romans 8:3:   . . . God, sending his own Son . . . .

Philippians 2:7:   . . . but made himself of no reputation . . . .

These three verses show the cooperation of the Spirit, the Father, and the Son in the Incarnation. Preexistence does not imply Deity, but Deity implies preexistence.

Then Berkhof continues with the important remark that "This also means that the incarnation was not something that merely happened to the Logos, but was an active accomplishment on his part."

If miracles, especially the miracle of the Virgin Birth, disturbed the Modernists of the late nineteenth and early twentieth centuries, Soren Kierkegaard, whose influence appeared in the United States only after Modernism began to wane, made more serious objections to the Incarnation itself. For him eternity is so antithetical to time that there is no possibility of the eternal becoming temporal. Later neo-orthodox theologians tried to preserve some contact between eternity and time by picturing eternity as a vertical line descending and cutting the horizontal time line at a point. Thus the eternal cuts time at a point. Since the intersection of two lines is a point, and has neither length, breadth, nor thickness, the contact between eternity and time has no temporal extension. Thus by a geometrical analogy (surely inappropriate to the material it claims to illustrate) the events of Jesus' ministry, three years in length, are reduced to triviality.

Before Barth's and Brunner's line that comes down *senkrecht von oben*, Kierkegaard himself wrote, "That God has existed in human form, has been born, grown up, and so forth is surely the paradox *sensu strictissimo*, the absolute paradox" *(Concluding Unscientific Postscript*, p. 194).

Kierkegaard does not use the term *paradox* in its ordinary English sense. In English a *paradox* is a charley-horse between the ears that can be eliminated by rational massage. But Kierkegaard makes it clear that if a paradox, in his sense, can be explained, it is not a paradox. A paradox is an absurdity to the understanding. He makes his irrationalism perfectly clear. He teaches that if God is not absurd, then we must accept pantheism rather than Christianity. Christian faith must be absurd. The Paradox is folly to the understanding. Such phrases and the whole tenor of this thought state his main contention that faith is contrary to reason. Logic is to be abandoned. The law of *Excluded Middle* and the law of *Contradiction* are denied in the Paradox of faith (compare *Concluding Unscientific Postscript*, pp. 189, 513). There can be no Trinity if God is rational. The Christian God must be absurd.

It is not easy to say how much attention a book on Christian doctrine should pay to these anti-Christian authors. Since they operate on pagan assumptions, it is not surprising that their inferences result in unbiblical conclusions. Even if their implications are valid, as they may often be, they cannot convince a Christian, for the Christian does not grant the premises. Even so, there is some utility in studying Kierkegaard and Barth. Because dialectical theology has been widely influential since World War II, the Christian should understand what it is that causes aberrations among some Christians and results in once-Christian seminaries departing the faith with itching ears. But besides this reason for knowing a little about neo-orthodoxy, there is another and more fundamental reason.

The aim of the orthodox theologian is of course to systematize what the Bible teaches. In doing so, however, there is always the possibility that we may make a mistake; and it is equally possible that our worst enemies will point it out. Therefore we have some responsibility to show that their objections apply neither to the Scriptures nor even to our systematization.

In this case it is not very difficult to dispose of Kierkegaard's objections. They do not apply to the Scriptural doctrine of the Incarnation. Kierkegaard thinks they do only because he does not understand the doctrine and misstates it in order to refute it. Of course it is impossible and absurd that the eternal be temporal. By mere tautology that which has no succession in time cannot *simpliciter* be that which has succession in time. But the Biblical doctrine asserts no such nonsense. Therefore Kierkegaard is wide of the mark.

The point in question is the impassibility of the divine nature. People today usually think that God has emotions. This vitiates all Christianity. It also indicates the low level to which personal Christianity has fallen since the eighteenth, not to mention the seventeenth, century. To indicate what the earlier, better educated Christians thought, I quote Augustus Toplady, the Anglican divine who wrote *Rock of Ages* and more than a hundred other hymns: "God is not irascible and appeasable, liable to emotions of joy and sorrow; or in any respect passive." Also: "when love is predicated of God, we do not mean that he is possessed of it as a passion or affection" (*Complete Works*, 1896, pp. 106, 107, 687).

Again Louis Berkhof is true to Scripture when he writes, "The divine nature did not undergo any essential change in the incarnation. This also means that it remained impassible, that is, incapable of suffering and death."[1] In other words the

---

1. Among true Christians today—I do not speak of the apostate denominations—

Christian position does not assert that a divine person became a human person. Even this is not tautologically absurd, for, although God cannot commit suicide, if a divine person became a human person he would not be both at the same time as Kierkegaard's absurdity requires. Much less does the Christian position assert this absurdity. Christ, as the Scripture references will soon show, was a divine person, the eternal Jehovah, the Wisdom, Power, and Logos of God; and while remaining what he was, associated with himself or assumed to himself, a complete human nature. Since this material appears most clearly in Jesus' life and ministry, the many details and the conclusions from them, by which Kierkegaard's misinterpretations are unmasked, will be postponed to the proper subsection.

There is, however, a thought that Kierkegaard's *Paradox* may suggest to a Bible student. Of course a Bible student might and even ought to think of it on his own, for even a minimum of consideration should give anyone some inkling of how stupendous the idea of the Incarnation is. Consider, consider: The Sovereign Eternal God, self-existent and self-sufficient, invisible, who dwells in light unapproachable and alone has immortality, the Almighty God, whose greatness is unsearchable, the blessed and only Potentate, beside whom there is no other, the first and the last, Alpha and Omega, the Omnipotent Creator, the only wise God, clothed with majesty, with honor, and with light as with a garment, who hath stretched out the heavens like a curtain, who sets his glory above the heavens, whose hand hath laid the foundation of the earth: heaven is his throne and earth his footstool; the King eternal, the King of Kings and Lord of Lords, the King of glory—When I consider thy heavens, the

there is a distressingly widespread ignorance of what God is. Of them it can be truly said that they have created God in their own image. In technical terms their religion is anthropocentric, not theocentric.

work of thy fingers, the moon and stars which thou hast ordained, what is man that thou art mindful of him and the son of man that thou visitest him? Consider: Why should the Most High make himself of no reputation, take upon himself the form of a servant, and be made in the likeness of men? Why?

Stupendous as all this is, there is an answer to the question. And it is not paradoxical absurdity.

6. The Virgin Birth

The New Testament explicitly asserts the "biological miracle" of the Virgin Birth.

Matthew 1:16, 18, 20, 23:	. . . Joseph, the husband of Mary, of whom was born Jesus . . . . When as his mother Mary was espoused to Joseph, before they came together, she was found with child of the Holy Ghost. . . . the angel of the Lord appeared unto him in a dream saying, Joseph, thou son of David, fear not to take unto thee Mary thy wife, for that which is conceived in her is of the Holy Ghost. . . . Behold a virgin shall be with child . . . .
Luke 1:34, 35:	Then said Mary to the angel, How shall this be, seeing that I know not a man? And the angel answered and said unto her, The Holy Ghost shall come upon thee, and the power of the Highest shall overshadow thee; therefore also that holy thing which shall be born of thee shall be called the Son of God.

Concerning these verses it may be noted that the relative *of whom* is feminine singular, and neither masculine nor plural. Matthew quotes the Old Testament prophecy about a virgin. Unbelieving scholars have tried to deny that the Hebrew word *almah* can mean *virgin*. Here two points may be noted: (1) There is no passage in the Old Testament where *almah* cannot mean virgin, though in one case the status of the girl is not made explicit; (2) Matthew translates *almah* as *parthenos*, and Matthew knew enough of both languages to translate it correctly. *Parthenos* must mean *virgin*. Then more conclusively, the Septuagint, translated by Alexandrian Jews more than a century before Christ, uses *parthenos* for *almah* in the passage Matthew quotes. Without crediting the accusation that Matthew distorted the Old Testament in order to favor Christianity, a Christian can reply that the Alexandrian Jews had no such prejudice. Nor can they be charged with an ignorance of Hebrew and Greek. Similarly in Genesis 24:43 the Septuagint translators used *parthenos* for *almah*; and surely Rebekah was a virgin. This argument is in no way weakened by the fact that the Septuagint also uses other words to translate *almah*.

One further point about Matthew and the destructive critics. It is the remarkable case of the Revised Standard Version. The New Testament was published separately a year or so before the Old Testament was completed. On its first page there is nothing suspicious. But when the entire Bible was published, and the first page of Matthew was not likely to be the first page a reader would look at, there appeared a footnote that had not been put in the New Testament edition. It stated: "Other ancient authorities read, Joseph to whom was betrothed the virgin Mary was the father of Jesus who is called Christ." It is amazing that unbelieving scholars should resort to such deceptive tactics. No *Greek* manuscript has such a reading. If *versions, i.e.*, translations, are authorities, there seems to be only one that makes Joseph the father of Jesus. And if there is only one, why did the Revised Standard Version say *authorities* in the plural? After believers protested that the note was a falsehood, the editors of the Revised Standard Version deleted the note from their later editions.

The passage quoted from Luke is even clearer than that in Matthew, if that were possible. One critic simply deleted Luke 1:35 from his translation. It is hard to account for such animosity. During the first third of this century candidates for ordination would sometimes express doubts about the Virgin Birth or deny outright such a "biological miracle." There is no Biblical reason for this opposition; nor is there any textual or exegetical reason. On philosophic grounds there is no more reason to reject the Virgin Birth than the Resurrection or any other miracle. If God is omnipotent, he can work miracles; if Scripture is God's revelation, he has worked miracles; and if critics reject supernaturalism, there is no use arguing with them about a single miracle. The real difficulty is their rejection of Christianity as a whole.

Aside from unbelieving enemies, friends within the Christian fold might ask, Why should there be a Virgin Birth anyhow? Why could not the Logos in his human nature have had two human parents? Would that not have made him more truly human? In answer to this question two reasons can be given and there may be others.

The first answer is that this was not the birth of a new person. Other births are births of new persons. No one who reads these words existed in 1850. Ordinary births require two parents; but the birth of a preexisting person is not ordinary. This consideration may not demonstrate the necessity of a virgin birth, but it sounds like a very good reason for expecting something unusual.

The second reason also may not be demonstrative, yet

there could be something to it. All ordinary babies suffer from total depravity because the guilt of Adam's sin is immediately imputed to them. Christ was sinless, he was not depraved, therefore the guilt of Adam's sin was not imputed to him at the time of his birth. Since the representative sin was the sin of a man, and not of a woman, it might have been more congruent for a sinless mediator to have a mother, but no father. This might not be *the* or even *an* explanation; but in a perfectly concatenated system there must be some relationship, and even a close relationship between the sinlessness of Christ and the non-imputation of Adam's sin. At any rate the New Testament teaches that Jesus was born of the Virgin Mary.

In connection with the Virgin Birth and even more so with the preceding section on the Incarnation, and also in anticipation of later implications, we may note that various theologians have asked whether these two related events were necessary. This question does not ask whether, under present actual conditions, it is necessary for us to believe in Christ's birth and death. The question is whether, before decreeing the actual plan of salvation, God could have chosen a different plan in which there would have been no Incarnation? Some theologians framed it this way: Is the idea of Incarnation involved simply in the idea of redemption, or was it antecedently involved in the idea of creation? Or it could be phrased: Would the Second Person of the Trinity have become incarnate even if man had not sinned? Some theologians argued that the Incarnation of a divine person is so stupendous that it must have been included in the very idea of any creation whatever. This reason, however, is transparently fallacious. Even if the work of Christ is more extensive than making atonement, it is by no means clear that he would have had to become incarnate in order to do it.

This problem is more complex than it seems at first, and we shall dig into it later. For the moment, however, let us remember that the Son of Man came, not to be ministered unto, but to give his life a ransom for many. He was named Jesus, for he was to save his people from their sins; and as the children are partakers of flesh and blood, he also took part of the same, for otherwise he could not have died. More of this later; much more.

7.   The Human Nature of Christ

Although the word *incarnation* means *coming into flesh*, this etymological sense is far from exhausting the doctrine. It is true that the preexisting eternal Jehovah became flesh or took a human body to himself; but apart from further New Testament instruction one could suppose, as some early Christians actually did, that the Logos simply took the place of a human soul in a human body. Or, again, since the idea of incarnation is so astounding and since it boggles the imagination to think of the eternal Jehovah's humiliating himself by becoming a man, one could suppose that the human body of Jesus was a phantom, a sort of ghost, a theophany, visible but unreal. On this particular point the account of the Virgin Birth is pertinent. The Old Testament theophanies were not born, virgin or otherwise. The subject of Christ's person and natures is a large one; the views held in early times were various and the debates were vigorous and even furious. The Patripassians or Sabellians, to quote Tertullian, "drove out the Paraclete and crucified the Father." In other words, God is one Person, not a Trinity of Persons; this one Person appears in three modes; therefore the Person who suffered on the cross was the Father in the guise of a Son. Apollinaris (A.D. 360) taught that the Logos in the visible Jesus took the place of the human soul as it is in ordinary man. Jesus was therefore true God, but not true man. The Nestorians (A.D. 430ff.) asserted both the Deity and the humanity of Christ, but claimed that he was two persons. Eutyches (*c.* A.D. 450) believed that the divine nature combined with a human nature so that the resulting combination was neither true God nor true man. The unity of the person, however, was strongly asserted.

In A.D. 451 the Council of Chalcedon met and adopted the Creed about to be quoted. Authoritatively settling some of these problems, though leaving some others in a state of ambiguity– or at least a non-explicit status–the Council set forth the doctrine that Christ is one Person with two natures:

> Following the holy fathers we teach with one voice that the Son and our Lord Jesus Christ is to be confessed as one and the same, that he is perfect in Godhead and perfect in manhood, very God and very man, of a reasonable soul and body, consubstantial with the Father as touching his Godhead, and consubstantial with us as touching his manhood; made in all things like unto us, sin only excepted; begotten of his Father before all worlds according to his Godhead, but in these last days for us men and for our salvation born of the Virgin Mary, the mother of God according to his manhood. This one and the same Jesus Christ, the only-begotten Son, must be confessed to be in two natures, unconfusedly, immutably, indivisibly, inseparably, and that without the distinction of natures being taken away by such union, but rather the peculiar property of each nature being preserved and being united in one Person and Hypostasis, not separated or divided into two persons, but one and the same Son and Only Begotten, God the Word, our Lord Jesus Christ, as the prophets of old time have spoken of concerning him, and as the Lord Jesus Christ hath taught us, and as the Creed of the fathers hath delivered to us.

The wording of this creed was very carefully chosen, and its implications cannot be seen without some study. Since that date the main body of professing Christians have mainly accepted Chalcedon. Though the present treatise is not particularly interested in history as such, we may insert the note that during the Reformation the Anabaptists seem to have taught that Christ brought his human nature with him at his incarnation and did not receive it through Mary. This is a rather queer idea in any case; besides which it interferes with his role as mediator.

The following verses are basic for an understanding of Christ's human nature.

Matthew 4:2:	And when he had fasted forty days and forty nights, he was afterward an hungered.
Matthew 26:38:	Then saith he unto them, My soul is exceeding sorrowful, even unto death: tarry ye here, and watch with me.
Mark 13:32:	But of that day and that hour knoweth no man, no, not the angels which are in heaven, neither the Son, but the Father.
Luke 2:52:	And Jesus increased in wisdom and stature, and in favour with God and man.
John 4:6:	Now Jacob's well was there. Jesus therefore, being wearied with his journey, sat thus on the well . . . .
John 8:40:	But now ye seek to kill me, a man that hath told you the truth, which I have heard of God: this did not Abraham.
John 11:35:	Jesus wept.
Acts 2:22:	Ye men of Israel, hear these words; Jesus of Nazareth, a man approved of God among you by miracles and wonders and signs, which God did by him in the midst of you, as ye your-

selves also know:

Hebrews 2:14:   Forasmuch then as the children are
                       partakers of flesh and blood, he also
                       himself likewise took part of the
                       same; that through death he might
                       destroy him that had the power of
                       death, that is, the devil;

II John 1:7:   For many deceivers are entered
                       into the world, who confess not that
                       Jesus Christ is come in the flesh. This
                       is a deceiver and an antichrist.

That there was a visible body, with flesh and bones, a body
that ate and drank, and walked here and there, hardly needs
further mention. The New Testament provides no basis at all for
supposing that Christ's body was any less real than the bodies of
Joseph, Mary, Peter, and Paul.

Note that the words just used are "any less real than the
bodies of Joseph, Mary, Peter, and Paul." This phraseology
by-passes the question as to whether or not Jesus had a
"material" body. Some theologians, orthodox enough, insist on
a "material" body. Now, it happens that many of these
theologians complain against authors who introduce Platonic
terminology into Christian doctrine. Yet these same theologians use and stress Aristotelian concepts, and surely Aristotle
was less religious than Plato. The concept of matter, as Aristotle
noted, had anticipations in early Greek philosophy; but it can
hardly be denied that Aristotle was the first to formulate a
definite concept. Even Democritus did not do so, though he
could properly be called a materialist. The question here is why
should various theologians so strongly insist on the concept of
one pagan philosopher while as strongly objecting to that of
another. This question has become more pertinent in the
twentieth century when science has largely, in fact entirely,

banished the concept of *matter* and replaced it with that of *energy*. I surmise that most college textbooks on Physics, published since 1925, hardly ever use the term *matter*. Now, then, rather than engaging in a debate between Newton and Einstein, it seems better to say that whatever *body* fundamentally is, Jesus had a body of the same composition as those of Mary and Peter.

What needs more emphasis is that Jesus had a human soul, and that the Logos was not its substitute. In other words, Christ was a man; he was not simplistically "God in a body" as a contemporary evangelist told his television audience. In modern times forces within the western religious community have attacked the Deity of Christ; and of course Islam and other eastern religions have always done so. But it is equally destructive of Christianity to deny Jesus' humanity. Such a denial makes Christ's mediatorial activity impossible and vitiates the doctrine of the Atonement. Hence one must pay attention to the Scriptural basis for asserting that Christ was a man, that is, in ordinary language, that he had a human soul.

Now, the verses quoted, in addition to showing that he walked here and there, also predicate of him psychological activities that are not possible of God. He got hungry, he got tired, he slept. But "he that keepeth Israel shall neither slumber nor sleep;" "the Creator of the ends of the earth fainteth not neither is weary." Jesus also experienced grief and sorrow. He called himself a man, and Peter called him a man. Deceivers and the antichrist deny that he came in the flesh; but since God's children are sharers in flesh and blood, he also himself *in like manner* partook of the same.

Luke 2 and Mark 13 assert his humanity in most extraordinary terms. As a boy Jesus grew in wisdom as well as in stature (neither of which Jehovah could do) and he even grew in favor with God as well as with men. In his adult life, during his ministry, he was ignorant of the date of his second advent. Presumably he was ignorant of other things as well; but the Logos is omniscient. The Scripture therefore attributes to Christ human psychological characteristics that cannot possibly be predicates of God.

But with all these finite creaturely characteristics so definitely asserted, it does not follow that the Messiah's essential deity was in any way impaired. In its insistence on Christ's human nature, the Bible does not teach what has come to be called the theory of Kenosis. This name is taken from

Philippians 2:5b-8:   Christ Jesus, who, existing in the form of God, counted not the being on an equality with God a thing to be grasped [at], but *emptied* himself [King James: made himself of no reputation] . . .

The verb *kenoō*, or the noun *kenōsis*, expresses the idea of *vain* or *empty*. The noun does not occur in the New Testament; the verb occurs five times: Romans 4:14 speaks of making faith *void*; I Corinthians 1:17 speaks of making the cross of Christ of *none effect*; in I Corinthians 9:15 Paul refers to something that would make his glorying *void*; in II Corinthians 9:3 it is boasting that should be *vain*; and Philippians 2:7 is the fifth instance. It would seem strange to translate this verse as "Christ made himself of none effect." He surely did not. There is nothing wrong with saying "Christ emptied himself," though it might be better to retain "made himself of no reputation;" and so far as translation goes, one could, with a minimum of stretching it, say "humbled himself."

All these translations need interpretation. The theory of Kenosis suffers from a certain degree of vagueness and from its modification in several authors. Henry Ward Beecher and others taught that the Logos so depotentiated himself of all his divine attributes that he completely ceased from his cosmic functions during the years of his earthly life. This view denies that the Logos took the place of the human soul and makes Christ, at least in his activity, entirely human. A variation of this holds that the Logos took the place of the human soul as it is in ordinary men, but that no divine prerogatives were exercised. Martensen is even more confused. Walter R. Martin wrote a small book for popular consumption, *Essential Christianity* (Zondervan, 1962, pp. 28-29) in which he says, "Christ did not exercise at least three prime attributes of Deity while on earth prior to his resurrection. These were Omniscience, Omnipotence, and Omnipresence." Henry C. Thiessen in his *Systematic Theology* describes the Kenosis theory as holding that "Christ emptied himself of his relative attributes—his omnipotence, omniscience, and omnipresence—while retaining his immanent attributes—his holiness, love, and truth." Then further down the page Thiessen continues, "Instead of the above mentioned theory, the Scriptures teach, when taken as a whole, that Christ merely surrendered the independent exercise of his relative attributes. He did not surrender the immanent attributes in any sense. . . . Thus he was omniscient as the Father granted him the exercise of these attributes."

This last view evinces considerable confusion. In the first place Thiessen (*Theology Proper*, III, "The Nature of God"), along with the Kenotists, uses the distinction between substance and attribute: ". . . By an attribute, in distinction from the substance of God, we mean 'any necessary predicate that can be applied to this essence . . . .' (Smith, *System of Christian Theology*, p. 12)." If, however, the distinction between substance and attribute be rejected as an Aristotelian imposition, the Kenotists and Thiessen also are both left with no foundation for their views.

In the second place, and a little more immediately pertinent to the "emptying" of Christ, the distinction between "relative" and "immanent" attributes is of little value. The Trinity, Christ included, was omniscient not only before his incarnation, but also in eternity apart from the created world. Omniscience therefore is not a mere relationship to creation. In fact, if the incarnate Christ retained his "immanent" attribute of truth, how could he fail to be omniscient? Similarly with omnipotence. God did not suddenly become potent or omnipotent upon creating the universe. Had God not created anything, he still would have been omnipotent. In the third place, the phrase "Christ merely surrendered the independent exercise of his relative attributes," even with the addition of "he was omniscient as the Father granted him the exercise of these attributes," is confusing. Even in eternity Christ's omniscience was not independent of the Father's omniscience. None of the Persons of the Trinity was ever independent. They are one God.

In the fourth place, the humiliation described in Philippians 2:7 is easily understood through the doctrine of the two natures of Christ. His human nature was never omniscient nor omnipotent. An omniscient, eternal nature just is not a human nature. And the divine Logos took to himself a human nature. But this second Person of the Trinity never ceased being the second Person. His Person, he himself, remained God. As God, or in his divine nature, he continued to "have" or exercise all the "attributes" he ever had. Consider these verses:

Matthew 11:27:   All things are delivered unto me of
                        my Father: and no man knoweth the
                        Son, but the Father; neither knoweth

any man the Father, save the Son, and he to whomsoever the Son will reveal him.

Matthew 18:20: For where two or three are gathered together in my name, there am I in the midst of them.

John 5:17: But Jesus answered them, My Father worketh hitherto, and I work.

John 8:58: Jesus said unto them, Verily, verily, I say unto you, Before Abraham was, I am.

John 10:30,38: I and my Father are one. But if I do, though ye believe not me, believe the works: that ye may know, and believe, that the Father is in me, and I in him.

I Corinthians 1:24: But unto them which are called, both Jews and Greeks, Christ the power of God, and the wisdom of God.

Ephesians 3:11: According to the eternal purpose which he purposed in Christ Jesus our Lord . . .

Colossians 2:2-3: That their hearts might be comforted, being knit together in love, and unto all riches of the full assurance of understanding, to the acknowledgement of the mystery of God, and of the Father, and of Christ; in whom are hid all the treasures of wisdom and knowledge.

Colossians 2:9: For in him dwelleth all the fulness of the Godhead bodily.

Hebrews 1:8-12: But unto the Son he saith, Thy throne, O God, is for ever and ever: a sceptre of righteousness is the sceptre of thy kingdom. Thou hast loved righteousness, and hated iniquity; therefore God, even thy God, hath anointed thee with the oil of gladness above thy fellows. And, Thou, Lord, in the beginning hast laid the foundation of the earth; and the heavens are the works of thine hands: They shall perish; but thou remainest; and they all shall wax old as doth a garment; and as a vesture shalt thou fold them up, and they shall be changed: but thou art the same, and thy years shall not fail.

Hebrews 13:8:   Jesus Christ the same yesterday, and to day, and for ever.

Matthew 11:27 asserts both omniscience and omnipotence, and especially the predestinating sovereignty of the Son in revealing himself to those whom he chooses. The Son's knowledge of the Father is put on a level with the Father's knowledge of the Son. That this equality of knowledge, and the predestinating sovereignty in revelation, is operative during Jesus' earthly ministry is clear in the fact that Jesus is referring to the successes and the failures of the evangelistic campaign of the seventy (compare Luke 10:17-22).

John 5:17, by itself, would be hardly sufficient to refute the theory of Kenosis. Any Christian minister can say, God works and I work too. But the context makes the working of the Father and the working of the Son so coextensive as to be inapplicable to any merely human evangelist. John 10:38 strengthens this disparity. Although there is a sense, a rather weak sense, in which God and the minister are one, for the sincere minister's purpose is imperfectly one with God's, it is rather hard for him to say that he is in the Father and the Father in him. Yet by itself, this sentence also can be interpreted, or misinterpreted, to apply.

The other verses are much more explicit in their denial of Kenosis, and with this denial the previous verses receive their proper weight. No sincere Christian pastor would claim to be the power of God and the wisdom of God. But does this show that the Incarnate Logos exercised these powers during Jesus' earthly ministry? Yes, it does; unless one wishes to claim that the Father had no power and wisdom for some thirty years. Nor is the reference to Christ's earthly ministry omitted from the context. Verse 18 mentions the cross, and verse 23 speaks of the crucifixion. One cannot maintain that Paul's identification of Jesus with the omnipotence of God is true only after the ascension.

Ephesians 3:11 might possibly be interpreted to mean that the plan of the ages was made in the Logos from eternity, but that the Logos lost the plan during his incarnation. This is not only a queer interpretation, but is also made less acceptable by the name of Jesus included in the sentence. Colossians 2:2-3 is similar to I Corinthians 1:24. What is probably the clearest verse is Colossians 2:9 where the apostle asserts that all the fulness of the Godhead dwells in Jesus bodily. It would not be all the fulness if even one attribute had been laid aside; and the term *bodily* can apply only to the incarnate Jehovah.

The two verses in Hebrews assert the immutability of Jesus Christ, yesterday, today during his earthly ministry, and forever.

But there is one other verse that is particularly interesting. John 1:9, along with 1:4, teaches that the epistemological abilities of every man who is born in the world result from Christ's activity. Since men were born and lived during Christ's earthly ministry, it follows that the populations of China, Africa,

and America were being enlightened by Christ even between 4
B.C. and A.D. 30. Jesus, during his earthly sojourn, never ceased
in any of his divine activities. But taking upon himself a human
nature was a humiliation.

This discussion of the Kenosis theory was introduced for
the purpose of defending the creed of Chalcedon to the effect
that the incarnate Person was both God and man. Neither one
without the other. The discussion has defended his full deity
during the time of his earthly ministry. But to conclude the
section on his humanity, there is one further and one all
important facet that demands full attention.

Christ is proved to be a man, not only because he got tired
and thirsty, but because he died. God cannot die. In fact it is
precisely because God cannot die that Jehovah became man.

8. The Purpose of the Incarnation

The purpose of the Incarnation therefore is that Jesus
should die. Even from the standpoint of secular history Jesus is
famous because he died. He is not famous because he was a
great moral teacher. Philosophers and teachers may become
famous if with intellectual ability they also live long enough.
Plato wrote and taught for about forty years; Aristotle for no
fewer. Schopenhauer is second rate because he stopped philoso-
phizing after he had written one great book. Can anyone think
of a great philosopher who taught for only three years? But
however it may be with the secular historians' evaluation of
greatness, the Scriptures say that Jesus' purpose in life was to
die. Otherwise there would have been no Incarnation at all.

Mark 10:45:   For the Son of Man also came . . .
                         to give his life a ransom for many.
John 12:27:   What shall I say? Father, save me

Hebrews 2:9,14:

from this hour? But for this cause came I unto this hour.

We behold . . . Jesus, because of the suffering of death, crowned with glory and honor, that by the grace of God he should taste death for every son . . . . Since then the children are sharers in flesh and blood, he also . . . partook of the same, that through death he might bring to nought . . . the devil.

These four verses state explicitly that Jehovah became incarnate in order to die. There are many others that imply this, even if the assertion is not explicit. For example, the angel told Joseph to name the child Jesus "for he shall save his people from their sins." Doubtless Joseph had no idea of how Jesus would save his people, but with our post-crucifixion knowledge we can see that this is a statement of purpose centering on his death. Similarly Mary could not then understand the meaning of "Yea, a sword shall pierce through thine own soul also;" but she understood later.

A little more explicit is

John 18:37:   To this end was I born, and for this cause came I into the world.

The immediately following words could be used to identify Jesus' purpose as teaching the truth, and the immediately preceding words as establishing a kingdom. Well, of course the Incarnation had a series of purposes: One states the literal truth in saying that God became incarnate in order to sit by a well in Samaria. But there is no way to eliminate the idea of death from the process in Pilate's court. Death is in verses 31, 32, and 19:6, 7, 10.

A more pervasive foundation for this theme is found in

Isaiah 53:7:   . . . as a lamb that is led to the
                                     slaughter . . .

compared with the identification of Jesus as that lamb in

John 1:29:   Behold the Lamb of God that tak-
                                     eth away the sin of the world.

Such passages summarize the significance of the Old
Testament ritual. The lamb was chosen to die. Christ was the
lamb chosen before the foundation of the world. Therefore he
came to die.

Furthermore, the idea of God's coming to earth and dying
is such an incongruent combination that if God really became
incarnate and actually died, we are compelled to conclude that
such a death must have been a major part of God's plan. Surely
God was not overwhelmed by Pilate's power: "Thou couldst
have no power at all against me, except it were given thee from
above." Therefore the necessity of the Incarnation lay in the
death of Christ. Jesus came to die.

Some theologians, among whom were Rothe, Dorner, and
Martensen, argued that such a stupendous event as the death of
God could not be contingent on the accidental and arbitrary act
of Adam's sin. If a mediator is necessary under actual present
conditions, a mediator must have been necessary before the fall.
But such an argument is not even plausible. Surely the need of a
mediator between a sinner and God does not imply such a need
between a sinless being and God. There is no Scriptural
evidence that Jesus is the mediator between God and the sinless
angels. Second, Adam's sin was not an accident or an arbitrary
act. When those theologians argue that the stupendous event of

the death of God must have been part of God's original plan, they indeed state the truth. But this in no way implies that the plan did not include Adam's sin, that this sin was an accident God somehow could not prevent, or that Christ's death was not directly related in the divine plan to the occurrence of sin in the human race. Creation is no more a part of the divine plan than is sin; and to relate the Incarnation to the former only rather than to the latter, or to some other divine necessity, as these theologians do, is a construction motivated by a rejection of the Scriptural doctrine of predestination.

It is awkward to speak of Adam's first sin as being "arbitrary" even from Adam's point of view, let alone from God's. Adam deliberately chose to live with Eve rather than to obey God and lose his lovely wife. If this is called arbitrary, there remains no difference between an arbitrary and a deliberate, purposive act.

It is hard to know what some theologians mean by *arbitrary*. In the case of human actions the *arbitrary* act may be an act of free will independent from God; and not only so, but also capricious, or unrelated to the agent's serious and constant concerns. In the case of God, since he is perfectly rational, none of his acts can be arbitrary. They all fit teleologically into a single universal plan. Later a section on the immediate imputation of Adam's sin to his natural posterity and of Christ's righteousness to the elect will further consider the question of arbitrary acts, for since God's will is sovereign, all his decrees are arbitrary.

At any rate the Scripture is clear. In addition to the previous verses one may use the following for the conclusion that Christ became incarnate in order to die.

Luke 19:10:   For the Son of man is come to seek
                               and to save that which was lost.

John 3:16:	For God so loved the world, that he gave his only begotten Son, that whosoever believeth in him should not perish, but have everlasting life.
Galatians 4:4-5:	But when the fulness of the time was come, God sent forth his Son, made of a woman, made under the law, to redeem them that were under the law, that we might receive the adoption of sons.
Philippians 2:8:	And being found in fashion as a man, he humbled himself, and became obedient unto death, even the death of the cross.
I John 3:8b:	For this purpose the Son of God was manifested, that he might destroy the works of the devil.

9. Active Obedience

Though the doctrine of active obedience concerns the details of Christ's earthly life, a biographical account—Strauss' *Leben Jesu,* Renan's *Vie de Jésus,* or more orthodox harmonies of the Gospels—is not essential to the present purpose. The essential is that in all historical or biographical details Jesus perfectly kept the law of God and was sinless.

| Isaiah 53:7,9: | . . . as a lamb that is led to the slaughter . . . although he had done no violence, neither was any deceit in his mouth. |
| Luke 1:35: | . . . wherefore also the holy thing which is begotten shall be called the Son of God. |

John 8:46:	Which of you convicteth me of sin?
II Corinthians 5:21:	. . . Him who knew no sin . . .
Hebrews 4:15:	. . . one that hath been in all points tempted like as we are, yet without sin.
Hebrews 7:26,27:	. . . holy, guileless, undefiled . . . who needeth not daily, like these priests, to offer up sacrifice, first for their own sins . . .
I Peter 1:19:	. . . with precious blood, as of a lamb without blemish and without spot . . .
I Peter 2:22:	. . . who did no sin . . .
I John 3:5:	. . . in him is no sin.

A few obvious remarks on these verses are sufficient to make the point. The Isaiah passage was used a few paragraphs above to show that Jesus came to die. But the passage also makes it clear, and I Peter 1:19 as well, that the lamb was without blemish, and no deceit was found in his mouth. Although the angel's statement in Luke that the baby to be born would be holy is not conclusive, for holy does not always mean sinless, the other verses so plainly assert the sinlessness of Christ that exegesis and explanation are supererogatory: "without sin," "who did no sin," "in him is no sin."

Sin is any transgression of or want of conformity unto the law of God. Since then Jesus is said to be without sin, he must have perfectly obeyed the law. This is called his active obedience in distinction from his suffering and death, which are his passive obedience, or, simply, his passion.

At this point the exposition of the doctrine of the Atonement strikes a snag. The first four sections, or at least sections two, three, and four, had their locus in eternity past; then

sections five to nine somewhat followed the life of Christ. Nor is
the historical account altogether illogical, for the life of Christ is
the outworking of the Covenants of Grace and Redemption.
The next historical event is the death of Christ. But this
presupposes an understanding of sin. Hence to preserve a
logical sequence it is necessary to return in history to the
Covenant of Works. Only afterward does the death of Christ
make sense.

10. The Covenant of Works

God made a Covenant of Works with Adam. Dispensationalists usually date the covenant of works from Moses to
Christ. The Scriptures describe it as having been made before
the Fall. The word *covenant* does not occur in the earliest
chapters of Genesis; but it is clear that God set forth certain
conditions that Adam had to fulfill. Unfulfillment meant death.
One may most plausibly suppose that, if death is the penalty for
disobedience, the reward of obedience would be life. This is
really more than a plausible supposition. It seems implied by the
ejection of Adam from the garden in order that he might not eat
of the tree of life. The tree of life, whose leaves and monthly
fruit are good, appears again in Revelation 22:2. Then in verse
14 the blessed are given the right to the tree of life in the
heavenly City. What Adam lost is here restored. One may
therefore conclude that the Covenant of Works contained both
a penalty and a reward. But because of one single sin the
Cherubim with their flaming sword prevented Adam from
eating. Had there been no sin, access to the tree would not have
been cut off. One single act brought the penalty.

But we proceed too rapidly. The express Scriptural basis
for asserting that there was such a covenant, and that any
infringement carried a penalty, must be given, at least in part.

This is all the more necessary here because the Arminians (early Methodists and present day Nazarenes) reject the penal theory of the Atonement. It is perfectly easy to show that Scripture assigns a penalty for a violation of the Covenant of Works; but the ease in finding verses to quote does not justify their omission.

The following are only a few verses that assert that sin carries a penalty.

Genesis 2:17:	. . . Thou shalt not eat of it, for in the day that thou eatest thereof, thou shalt surely die.
Genesis 4:10ff.:	. . . The voice of thy brother's blood crieth unto me from the ground . . . And Cain said unto the Lord, My punishment is greater than I can bear. . . . Everyone that findeth me shall slay me. . . . And the Lord set a mark on Cain . . . .
Genesis 6:7,13:	And the Lord said, I will destroy man. . . . for the earth is filled with violence. . . . I will destroy them with the earth.
Genesis 9:6:	Whoso sheddeth man's blood, by man shall his blood be shed; for in the image of God made he man.
Genesis 15:12,14:	An horror of great darkness fell upon him. And he said unto Abram, . . . that nation whom they shall serve, will I judge.
Exodus 21:12ff.:	He that smiteth a man, so that he die, shall be surely be put to death. . . . He that smiteth his father or his mother shall be surely put to death. He that stealeth a man. . . . he that

curseth his father or his mother shall
surely be put to death. . . . Eye for eye,
tooth for tooth, hand for hand, foot for
foot.

Numbers 16:32,35:

And the earth opened her mouth
and swallowed them up, and their
houses, and all the men that apper-
tained unto Korah and all their goods
. . . And there came out a fire from the
Lord, and consumed the two hundred
and fifty men that offered incense.

I Samuel 2:22ff.:

Now Eli was very old, and heard all
that his sons did unto all Israel. . . .
And he said unto them, Why do ye
such things, for I hear of your evil
dealings by all this people? . . . If a
man sin against the Lord, who shall
entreat for him? Notwithstanding,
they hearkened not unto the voice of
their father, because the Lord would
slay them. And there came a man of
God unto Eli, and said unto him. . . .
Behold the days come that I will cut
off thine arm . . . and thou shalt see an
enemy in my habitation. . . . there
shall not be an old man in thine house
for ever. . . . Hophni and Phineas, in
one day, they shall die both of them.

In the first of these verses death is established as the
penalty for sin. Genesis four presupposes not only capital
punishment for murder, but also that Cain's brothers knew of
this penalty and were aware of their right to impose it. However,
for some reason not fully spelled out, God spared Cain. After

the flood had wiped out the race, the principle of capital punishment was made explicit to Noah. The revelation to Abram included a penalty to be imposed on Egypt. Exodus specifies the death penalty for a series of crimes. The passage in Numbers describes the death of three rebels and two hundred and fifty of their followers. Not to lengthen the list from Joshua through Judges, nor to continue throughout the Old Testament, the prediction of disaster on Eli's house forever, beginning with the death of his sons, is sufficient as a conclusion at this point. Note here that God had ordained the sons' refusal to hearken to their father's final rebuke because God intended to kill them.

These verses, however, do not make it very clear whether or not evil men suffer a penalty after death. The sinner is executed, but nothing further is said. Although the results of sin in a future life are still not clear, these verses show a provision for redemption; and perhaps the idea of redemption, the idea of being cleansed from sin, and therefore of standing righteous before God, intimates a future blessedness, even if it does not certify a future penalty. Other verses say more, and there now follows a condensation of

Exodus 29:10-37:   And thou shalt cause a bullock to be brought before the tabernacle of the congregation; and Aaron and his sons shall put their hands upon the head of the bullock. And thou shalt kill the bullock before the Lord. . . . and thou shalt take of the blood of the bullock and put it upon the horns of the altar. . . . It is a sin offering. Thou shalt also take one ram . . . and thou shalt slay the ram, and thou shalt take his blood and sprinkle it round about upon the altar. . . . And thou shalt offer every

day a bullock for a sin offering for
atonement; and thou shalt cleanse the
altar, when thou hast made an atonement for it. . . . It shall be an altar
most holy; whatsoever toucheth the
altar shall be holy.

These verses may be taken as representative of all similar
provisions in the Levitical law. It is not the present purpose to
read into them the full New Testament explanation of them as
anticipatory of Christ and his sacrifice. Rather one should first
determine their minimal meaning—the meaning that a fairly
devout Israelite of that age could be expected to discern with a
little thoughtfulness. The words, "it is a sin offering," indicate
that somehow and to some extent these offerings restore the
sinner to God's favor. They remove from him the necessity of
suffering the penalty himself. Obviously they presuppose that
sin carries a penalty; and this is the important point just now.

The effects in a future life are not too clear. Yet if God is the
eternal sovereign, the Maker of heaven and earth, the creator of
mankind, the gracious consoler of Eve in giving her a son, Seth,
to replace Abel, and a line through Enos, which, contrasted with
the Cainites, would fear God and produce a man Enoch, who so
walked with God that God took him, if too God in the Levitical
Law provides an atonement and holiness—if all this is so, could
not a fairly devout Israelite of Moses's day surmise that anyone
cleansed by the atoning sacrifice would enjoy God's favor in a
future world? The liberal theologians of the nineteenth and
twentieth centuries, who can find no hint of immortality in the
Old Testament, do not qualify as devout Israelites of Moses's
day.

The New Testament, of course, is more, much more
explicit.

Matthew 3:7:	. . . O generation of vipers, who hath warned you to flee from the wrath to come?
Matthew 5:22:	. . . whosoever shall say, Thou fool, shall be in danger of hell fire.
Matthew 5:29:	. . . it is profitable for thee that one of thy members should perish, and not that thy whole body should be cast into hell. (See also verse 30.)
Matthew 8:12:	But the children of the kingdom shall be cast into outer darkness: there shall be weeping and gnashing of teeth.
Matthew 10:28:	. . . rather fear him that is able to destroy both soul and body in hell.
Matthew 13:42:	His angels . . . shall cast them into a furnace of fire: there shall be wailing and gnashing of teeth. (See also verse 50.)
Matthew 18:8:	It is better for thee to enter into life halt or maimed, rather than having two hands or two feet to be cast into everlasting fire. (See also verse 9.)
Matthew 25:46:	These shall go away into everlasting punishment: but the righteous into life eternal.

In these verses from Matthew the advance over the Old Testament verses consists in the very clear statement that the penalty for sin is everlasting, as everlasting as eternal life; and also in the more explicit description of how terrible that punishment shall be. Not to repeat these ideas from Mark and Luke, only one verse from John will complete the Gospels; to which one verse from Acts will be added before giving a list from the remainder of the New Testament.

John 3:36:   He that believeth not the Son shall
                                    not see life; but the wrath of God
                                    abideth on him.

Acts 13:46:   . . . seeing ye put it [the word of
                                    God] from you, and judge yourselves
                                    unworthy of everlasting life, lo, we
                                    turn to the Gentiles.

The first of these two verses speaks of the wrath of God.
Following verses will add to this idea of wrath. The verse from
Acts is just one of a great number which, in one way or another,
imply that there is punishment of sin. Now come some of the
most important verses from the epistles:

Romans 1:18:   The wrath of God is revealed from
                                    heaven against all ungodliness and
                                    unrighteousness of men.

Romans 1:32:   Who, knowing the judgment of
                                    God, that they which commit such
                                    things are worthy of death, not only
                                    do the same, but have pleasure in
                                    them that do them.

Romans 5:9:   We shall be saved from wrath
                                    through him.

Romans 6:21:   . . . the end of those things is
                                    death.

Ephesians 5:6:   . . . because of these things cometh
                                    the wrath of God upon the children of
                                    disobedience.

Philippians 3:19:   . . . whose end is destruction . . .

I Thessalonians 1:10:   . . . Jesus, who delivered us from
                                    the wrath to come.

II Thessalonians 1:7-9:   . . . the Lord Jesus shall be revealed
                                    from heaven with his mighty angels,
                                    in flaming fire taking vengeance on

	them that know not God and that obey not the gospel of our Lord Jesus Christ; who shall be punished with everlasting destruction . . .
II Peter 2:4,9:	For if God spared not the angels who sinned, but cast them down to hell . . . . the Lord knoweth how to deliver the godly out of temptations, and to reserve the unjust unto the day of judgment to be punished.
II Peter 3:7:	. . . reserved unto fire against the day of judgment and perdition of ungodly men.
Revelation 20:15:	Whosoever was not found written in the book of life was cast into the lake of fire.

The immediate point of all these verses is that God has decreed a penalty for sin. Sin is the lack of conformity unto or transgression of the law of God. Toward such disobedience God exhibits his wrath. No understanding of the Atonement is possible without a conception of divine wrath. This term occurred in four of the verses just quoted; the term *vengeance* occurred once; *punish, judgment, perdition, everlasting destruction*, and *lake of fire*, all are found. These threats and warnings are directed against *ungodliness* (twice), *disobedience* (twice), the *unjust*, and those not found *in the book of life*. All this constitutes a penal theory of sin and must therefore require a penal theory of Atonement.

11. The Vicarious Sacrifice

Christ by dying suffered a penalty for sin instead of our suffering the penalty that was due us. Verses have already been quoted to show that God imposes on man a penalty for sin. Dozens of other verses could also be quoted. The present section will show that Christ was our substitute. This is a most important idea, and although not all pertinent verses will be quoted, a list a little longer than usual is justified.

John 1:29:   . . . Behold the Lamb of God, which taketh away the sin of the world.

Matthew 20:28:   Even as the Son of man came not to be ministered unto, but to minister, and to give his life a ransom for many.

I Corinthians 5:7b: . . . for even Christ our passover is sacrificed for us.

II Corinthians 5:14:   For the love of Christ constraineth us; because we thus judge, that if one died for all, then were all dead.

Galatians 3:13:   Christ hath redeemed us from the curse of the law, being made a curse for us: for it is written, Cursed is every one that hangeth on a tree.

Ephesians 5:2:   And walk in love, as Christ also hath loved us, and hath given himself for us an offering and a sacrifice to God for a sweetsmelling savour.

Hebrews 9:28:   So Christ was once offered to bear the sins of many; and unto them that look for him shall he appear the second time without sin unto salvation.

I Peter 2:24:   Who his own self bare our sins in his own body on the tree, that we, being dead to sins, should live unto righteousness: by whose stripes ye were healed.

I Peter 3:18:   For Christ also hath once suffered
                                       for sins, the just for the unjust, that he
                                       might bring us to God, being put to
                                       death in the flesh, but quickened by
                                       the Spirit.

    John 1:29 recalls not only Isaiah 53, but also passages such
as Leviticus 1:4 and 16:21, 22 where the idea of substitution is
unmistakably expressed. The verse from Matthew and its
parallel in Mark 10:45 put the idea of substitution in the
preposition *anti*, instead of. Matthew 2:22 says that Archelaus
was reigning *anti*, in the place of, his father Herod. Some other
verses, *e.g.*, II Corinthians 5:14, use the preposition *huper;* this is
a word of wider meaning and can be translated as *in behalf of*
without necessarily requiring substitution. For example, suppose a pastor is sick or on vacation. A visitor takes his place.
This visiting minister preaches *for* the absent pastor and he also
preaches *for* the congregation. But the preposition *for* has two
different meanings in these two expressions. The visitor
preaches *instead of* the pastor; he preaches *on behalf of* or *for the
good of* the congregation. The Greek *huper* is similar to the
English *for*. When the liberals used to claim that *huper* could
not possibly mean *instead of*, they were wrong. More recent
studies of papyri show that *huper* was used by a stenographer or
professional scribe who wrote for and instead of his employer.
Hence the wider *huper* in II Corinthians 5:14 does not weaken
the unambiguous *anti* in Matthew 20:28. In I Corinthians 5:7
the preposition is again *huper;* but the important point is that
Christ's death is said to be our Passover sacrifice. This makes
Christ's death as substitutionary as any of the Old Testament
lambs. Since too the Old Testament lambs had to be without
spot or blemish, so too Christ had to be sinless by virtue of his

active obedience. Substitution and sinlessness have a direct bearing also on expiation of sin and propitiation of God, for the doctrine of the Atonement is a closely knit complex of ideas.

One of these ideas, in Mark 10:45 with its preposition *anti*, is that of a ransom. It is worthy of a paragraph or two—to put it mildly. Single verses often have a bearing on several topics. The verse in Mark, and likewise in Matthew 20:28, as if it were necessary to defend its genuineness against destructive critics, can be used to show the purpose of the Incarnation, discussed and quoted here in section eight. Christ's death was not an unforeseen accident that obstructed his plan: It was a part, a major part, of that plan. But in addition to this, the verse clarifies the method of the plan. It was the payment of a ransom. As part of the plan the death must be viewed as a voluntary transaction, not as an involuntary martyrdom. This idea is again plainly stated in Christ's bold reply to Pilate, "Thou couldst have no power against me at all, except it were given thee from above."

But let us center on the idea of a ransom. Ordinarily a ransom is a sum of money paid to a slave-holder or to a military authority for the liberation of a slave or hostage. The subject is redeemed. The Old Testament has several references to such a redemption (Exodus 21:30; Leviticus 19:20 and 25:51; Isaiah 45:13). But no ransom was applicable to the liberation of a murderer (Numbers 35:31,32). In addition to such civil circumstances the Old Testament speaks of ransoms paid to God through his priestly representatives (Numbers 3:49 and 18:15; Psalms 107:2; *et al.*). These payments averted the divine displeasure. In some of these cases the person himself paid the ransom; in other cases another paid; and in Christ's case he paid the ransom instead (*anti*) of our paying it.

Although the civil ransoms, and even the religious ransoms in the Old Testament, were payments of money, the ransom paid for our redemption from the penalties of sin was nothing less than Christ's death on the cross. "He came to give his life a ransom for many."

This material, discussed by virtually every theologian, is so familiar that it can be included here only under the excuse of relative completeness. The interweaving of elements of the Atonement is found in most of the references. Not to exegete every one quoted just above, we may note that substitution and as well the idea of penalty are clear in Galatians 3:13. Christ became a curse for us and so redeemed us from the curse or penalty of the law, the penalty that otherwise we should have to bear ourselves; and finally it may be sufficient to point out the pointed language of the two verses from I Peter. Christ bore *our* sins in *his own* body . . . the just for the unjust.

The volumes on Systematic Theology usually explain and refute other views of the Atonement. The debate has slackened today, if I am not mistaken, because those who reject it no longer attempt to claim that their substitutes are Scriptural. They openly deny inerrancy so that it makes no difference to them what the Bible says. However, a Christian has a better understanding and a better preparation for publishing the glad tidings, if he has some knowledge of the earlier controversies. The following will be only a reminder, hardly a summary, and certainly not a history of the doctrine.

One, perhaps the most obvious, objection to a vicarious atonement is the principle that the punishment of a crime must be imposed on the criminal and cannot be justly imposed on any substitute. Berkhof gives a miserable answer to this objection. He states, what is true enough, that in ordinary life "the innocent often suffer as a result of the transgression of others" (p. 378). Of course! If someone robs you, you suffer as a result of his crime. But you do not suffer as a penalty for his crime. No one would argue that you should be put into jail because you are the victim of a burglary.[1] Berkhof further adds that "One who hires another to commit a crime is held responsible." But did Christ hire us to commit a crime for him? Were we his agents in sin? Nonsense. But even Hodge uses this argument: "Where is the propriety of saying that the innocent cannot suffer justly for the guilty, when we see that they actually do thus suffer continually, and everywhere since the world began?" (Charles Hodge, *Systematic Theology*, Vol. II, p. 530). But we do not see that they suffer justly. We see only that they suffer, and we regularly regard them as having suffered unjustly. A much better answer, and a satisfactory one, in my opinion, combines the idea of federal headship and the sovereignty of God, which two will be discussed in sections 15 and 18 below.

The Socinians, a sixteenth century group whom we would call Unitarians today, denied that Christ's death was a ransom. The term *ransom*, like the parables, is figurative and designates at most a single point of similarity. Both in religion and after a war prisoners are released; but nothing is implied as to the method or considerations for a release. In the case of Christ's death the effect is to inspire us to live a more self-sacrificing life. On this basis, or on no basis at all, God in his goodness can forgive us. This view, however, stumbles over its own feet because the only point of similarity in the verse is the idea of ransom. The term *ransom* does not in strictness mean *deliverance*. It designates the *method* of deliverance. If anything in the passage is literal, it is *ransom* itself.

So much for the verse itself; but the verse is embedded in a more extensive scriptural background. This background includes, includes very definitely, the doctrine of the Trinity. If Christ were a mere man, and not God, his death might very well

---

1. Some left-wingers might so argue, for they hold society responsible, while the criminal is supposed to be merely sick.

be nothing more than an edifying example. This is of course what the Socinians believed. They were Unitarians. But if Scripture teaches the deity of Christ, it must also teach that his death was no simple example. Hence a scriptural defense of the Trinity is also a scriptural defense of a substitutionary sacrifice. They go together, and the Socinians deny both. On this point the Socinians cannot be charged with inconsistency: They can be charged with a rejection of Scripture. Let this suffice as an example of objections that have been raised against the scriptural doctrine.

12. Expiation

Although lengthy exegesis of the verses just above is not necessary in order to establish the idea of substitution, substitution is not the whole story. For one thing, not all substitutionary sacrifices are penalties. When a pinch hitter, substituting for a less dependable player, makes a sacrifice bunt, he is not discharging any penalty previously imposed on the regular batter. In a mine disaster where the conditions are such that only one of the two men can get out alive, a single man might sacrifice his life for a father with several children. It is substitution, but not penalty. Christ's death, however, was a penalty.

In the previous list of verses Galatians 3:13 contained the idea of penalty. The curse of the law is the death penalty the law inflicts. Christ became that penalty, or took that curse, for us. Hebrews 9:28, enforced by all the other Old Testament references, pictures Christ as offered up to God in sacrifice bearing the sins of many. This epistle was written primarily to Jews. Not only chapter nine, but much else in the other chapters reminded the Jews of the Old Testament sacrifices and penalties for sin: Surely he hath borne our griefs; he was wounded for our transgressions; and the chastisement or penalty of our salvation was upon him, for with his stripes we are healed.

Expiation means the canceling of sin, purging it out, washing it away, covering it up (though not in the contemporary pejorative sense). It is common to speak of expiating a crime by paying the penalty. The English word *expiate* apparently does not occur in the King James version, but the Bible is full of expressions describing the purging away of sins. These are expiated, not by serving a term in jail, but by the shed blood of Christ. First, some verses describe the Old Testament anticipations; second, the New Testament asserts the reality anticipated.

Leviticus 1:4:	And he shall put his hand upon the head of the burnt offering; and it shall be accepted for him to make atonement for him.
Leviticus 4:3,4:	If the priest that is anointed do sin according to the sin of the people; then let him bring for his sin, which he hath sinned, a young bullock without blemish unto the Lord for a sin offering; and he shall bring the bullock unto the door of the tabernacle of the congregation before the Lord; and shall lay his hand upon the bullock's head, and kill the bullock before the Lord. (Compare the remainder of the chapter, and also chapter 16.)
Leviticus 17:11:	For the life of the flesh is in the blood; and I have given it to you upon the altar to make an atonement for your souls; for it is the blood that maketh an atonement for the soul.

John 1:29:

The next day John seeth Jesus coming unto him, and saith, Behold the Lamb of God which taketh away the sin of the world.

Romans 5:9:

Much more then, being now justified by his blood, we shall be saved from wrath through him.

Hebrews 1:3:

. . . Who being the brightness of his glory, and the express image of his person, and upholding all things by the word of his power, when he had by himself purged our sins, sat down on the right hand of the Majesty on high;

Hebrews 9:26:

For then must he often have suffered since the foundation of the world; but now once in the end of the world hath he appeared to put away sin by the sacrifice of himself. (Compare 10:4-14.)

I John 1:7:

But if we walk in the light, as he is in the light, we have fellowship one with another, and the blood of Jesus Christ his Son cleanseth us from all sin.

Revelation 7:14-15:

And I said unto him, Sir, thou knowest. And he said to me, These are they which came out of great tribulation, and have washed their robes, and made them white in the blood of the Lamb. Therefore are they before the throne of God, and serve him day and night in his temple: and he that sitteth on the throne shall dwell among them.

The idea that somehow or other man's sin is expiated is so clearly stated in these verses that there is hardly a possibility that other language can state it more clearly; and not merely "somehow or other," but in one definite way; for, to use one example, Hebrews 1:3 says that Christ purged our sins. It was his work, not ours. But though the basic idea is so clear, a point or two can be noted that may have escaped the careless reader. Expiation is not a moral improvement of the sinner. When in human affairs a man expiates his sin by a term in jail, this does not necessarily, nor even usually, make him a better man. What his incarceration does is to free him from any further penalty. Similarly, when Christ paid our penalty, we are freed from any further penalty. If *guilt* means liability to punishment, expiation removes that liability. Paying the penalty may or may not induce moral improvement; it does not remove defilement or depravity; it cancels the guilt—that is all.

Though expiation is such a simple idea that it requires little explanation, it is one of the most important in preaching the gospel to unsaved sinners. They need to know that their sins can be forgiven, washed away, no longer imputed to them. Hence a few more words on the subject may give it a needed emphasis.

To put it in proper pulpit style, the text might be "Jesus took bread, and having given thanks and blessed it, he broke it. . . . after supper he took the cup . . . and said, Drink ye all of it . . . this cup is the new covenant in my blood, which is shed for many for the remission of sins." These words, with slight variation, occur in Matthew 26:26; Mark 14:22; and Luke 22:19.

Here Christ called his blood a covenant, thus bringing into focus all the Old Testament had taught about the covenant. It is difficult to stick very closely to the subject, for all Scripture is interwoven, and one passage needs explanation from another.

Not only may one refer to the Old Testament here, one may also refer to all that the epistle to the Hebrews says about the covenant. Without disparaging Christ's teaching ministry, this institution of the Lord's Supper indicates that for all ages to come his death will be commemorated. There was something in his death that his teaching could not do. That something was the remission of sins.

Once more, the blood shed for the remission of sins takes us back to the Old Testament sacrifices.[1] Moses instructed the Israelites to kill a lamb and to sacrifice it. It was a sacrifice made to God. Possibly many of those ancient Jews did not understand that their sacrifice prefigured a later and more perfect sacrifice. Possibly, and as time went on probably, the more devout worshippers surmised that their current sacrifices foreshadowed a greater one. In any case the sacrifice brought the forgiveness of sins. With this background Jesus told his disciples that his shed blood would purge away their sins. His death is the cause and remission is the effect.

This rules out any moral influence theory of atonement. Moral influence is not atonement in any case. Moral influence may indeed in some cases result in one's improving his own life. Young men are often so inspired by the conduct of some hero that they want to emulate him, in science, in scholarship, in politics, or even in baseball. Possibly Renan and Bushnell were stimulated to imitate Jesus' example of gentleness and love. But Christ's death is first of all directed toward the cancellation of one's past life, and only afterward to the improvement of one's future days. Its purpose was the forgiveness of sins. Moral influence forgives nothing.

Of course expiation is not all there is to the doctrine of the

---

1. Compare Charles Hodge, *Systematic Theology*, Vol. II, pp. 501-508.

Atonement. The next point is perhaps the most important part of this central doctrine of the Bible.

13. Propitiation

This most important element in the doctrine of the Atonement is without doubt the element which heretics the most vigorously hate. H.B. Smith, (*System of Christian Theology*, p. 437, note), makes a pertinent introductory observation:

> A writer who became prominent as a controversialist on this subject, wrote, some years ago, "Every tyro in theology knows or ought to know that atonement means nothing more than at-one-ment, that is, the reconciliation of opposing parties." But none but a tyro in theology knows that this is its only sense. Even admitting the correctness of the etymology, it must be said that this way of reducing the large import of language to the smallest possible dimensions, by means of etymology alone, and of deciding theological controversies by an appeal to the primitive sense of words before they had gained their full signification is one unworthy of the scholar and theologian. All the etymology in the world would never be sufficient to show that atonement means only reconciliation—for the very plain reason that for hundreds of years it has borne in the English language an additional sense, that is, it includes a designation of the mode in which the reconciliation was affected ... the doctrine of expiation, atonement, or satisfaction, made by Christ in his blood.

Not only has the English word *atonement* designated a mode in which reconciliation has been effected, but the desire to understand that mode has motivated intelligent Christians from the days of the apostles to the present. One of the first attempts, however seriously put forward, seems strangely perverse now. Starting from the undeniable fact that sin brought the human race under the power of Satan, and looking at the verse which says Christ's death is a ransom, many early theologians, not including Athanasius, held that Christ's death was that ransom paid to the devil. Such was the view of Irenaeus, Origen, Gregory of Nyssa; but Gregory of Nazianzus calls it blasphemy, and Hilary even states that Christ's death was a penal satisfaction offered to God. Yet Ambrose a few years later continued the idea of a ransom to the devil. This probably explains why Augustine made some use of this early doctrine. At any rate, it was a widely received view. But though Augustine says a few things that sound like the early doctrine, his remarks are more vague, and other ideas on the atonement supervene.

Anselm (1109), who, though still possessed by the superstitions about penance from early times, with great originality began to grasp the concept of satisfaction and explicitly rejected satisfaction of the devil. Abelard (1142) sharpened these arguments: (1) Christ redeemed only the elect, and these were never in the devil's power; (2) if the devil seduced man, this gives him no right over man, but makes him deserving of punishment; and (3) the devil could not give man the immortality he promised, and so again could have no rights over him. "By these reasons," says Abelard, "it seems convincingly proved that the devil had . . . no rights against man . . . except perhaps [by] . . . the permission of the Lord who had given man over to him as jailer or torturer for punishment" (Migne, II, col. 834).

These ideas were hard for men of those times to assimilate. Bernard of Clairvaux (1153), a muddle-headed mystic, reverted to the earlier view. In opposition to Abelard he asserted that redemption by a ransom paid to the devil is a doctrine which all doctors since the apostles agree upon. Let Abelard know that the devil not only had a power, but a just power over men. Man was justly held captive by him [and God was under obligation to pay off the devil].

The history is interesting; and unless it had thus occurred, we today might have been as puzzled as, perhaps not Bernard, but Augustine. The aim now is to show that Christ's death was a sacrifice to satisfy the justice of God. In other words, Christ's death was a propitiatory sacrifice. The word itself—propitiation—is not of frequent occurrence; but it occurs and cannot be disregarded.

Romans 3:25:	Whom God hath set forth to be a propitiation through faith in his blood, to declare his righteousness for the remission of sins that are past, through the forbearance of God;
Hebrews 2:17:	Wherefore in all things it behooved him to be made like unto his brethren, that he might be a merciful and faithful high priest in things pertaining to God, to make reconciliation for the sins of the people.
I John 2:2:	And he is the propitiation for our sins: and not for ours only, but also for the sins of the whole world.
I John 4:10:	Herein is love, not that we loved God, but that he loved us, and sent his son to be a propitiation for our sins.

These four verses all use the word, verb or noun, *propitiate*. The verb in Hebrews is *ilaskesthai* and should not have been translated *reconcile*. The New American Standard has it correctly: *propitiation*. There are also about ten occurrences of another word translated *reconcile*. Since the latter is not a precise synonym, attention will be restricted to the former. Yet it must be understood that the doctrine of propitiation is not based on these verses alone. Behind them stand the Biblical propositions on the wrath of God—an unpopular topic but indispensable to Biblical religion.

Matthew 3:7:	. . . who hath warned you to flee from the wrath to come?
John 3:36:	. . . but the wrath of God abideth on him.
Romans 1:18:	For the wrath of God is revealed from heaven. . .
Romans 2:5,8:	. . . wrath against the day of wrath . . . indignation and wrath. (Compare Romans 4:15, 5:9, 9:22.)
Ephesians 2:3:	. . . the children of wrath . . .
Ephesians 5:6:	. . . because of these things cometh the wrath of God upon the children of disobedience. (Compare Colossians 3:6.)

Now, propitiation is some process or other by which the anger or wrath of one person toward another is dissipated. To propitiate means to turn wrath aside; to reconcile; to make a person favorably disposed.

The first meaning listed in Liddell and Scott is *to appease*. The second translation is *to conciliate*. The third is its particular and peculiar use in Hebrews 2:17. There is no preposition following the verb and one might think of translating it as "to propitiate the sins of the people." But *sins* are *expiated*; *God* is *propitiated*. However, it is equally true that *sins* are not *reconciled*. Therefore in either case a preposition must be inserted in English; and thus the New American Standard is justified in translating it "make propitiation *for* the sins of the people."

In the Old Testament the repentant worshipper offered the

sacrifice of a lamb.[1] The burning of the designated parts of the lamb on the altar was not primarily intended to produce any psychological change in the worshipper. The change called repentance had occurred before the sacrifice was offered. After the sacrifice the worshipper might experience a feeling of relief or forgiveness; but this could happen only because he believed that God had accepted his sacrifice and had turned aside his anger from him. Thus the primary aim of the sacrifice was to appease God's wrath and to reconcile him to oneself.

Nearly all Americans know the name of the great Jewish holy day, Yom Kippur, the Day of Atonement. In Hebrew the word has several forms: *kāpar, kōper, kappōret.* One meaning of this root is *ransom.* To quote the *Theological Wordbook of the Old Testament* (Harris, Archer, and Waltke, Vol. I, p. 453),

> Every Israelite was to give to the service of the sanctuary the "ransom" money of half a shekel. . . . This word "ransom" is parallel to the word "redeem" (*pādâ,* which see) in Ps 49:7. There is a warning that a man guilty of murder must be killed—no "ransom" can be given in exchange for his life. . . . [*Kāpar*] . . . means "to atone by offering a substitute" . . . the priestly ritual of sprinkling of the sacrificial blood. . . . The verb is always used in connection with the removal of sin or defilement, except for Gen 32:20; Prov 16:14; and Isa 28:18 where the related meaning of "appease by a gift" may be observed. . . . The life of the sacrificial animal specifically symbolized by its blood was required in exchange for the life of the worshipper. . . . the symbolic expression of innocent life given for guilty life. This symbolism is further clarified by the

---

1. B.B. Warfield, *Biblical Doctrines* (Oxford University Press, 1929, pp. 405-411), gives a detailed analysis of the sacrifices of Cain and Abel, noting clearly the different motivations of the two men.

action of the worshipper in placing his hands on the head of the sacrifice and confessing his sins over the animal . . . .

See also the paragraphs on *kippūr* and *kappōret.*

It can hardly be denied that the Old Testament is the background of the New. Indeed the New Testament would be unintelligible without the Old. Hence when the New Testament writers spoke of Christ's death as a sacrifice, what else could they have possibly meant except an expiatory death to propitiate God and to reconcile him to our guilty selves?

It is now humorous, but still instructive, to note a reviewer's defense of Bousset's *Religion of Judaism* to the effect that it contains no exposition of the Jewish theory of sacrifice "because there wasn't any." In this century our enemies mostly agree that the Scriptures teach what we have always said they teach. This phase of nineteenth century liberalism is defunct.

That the New Testament is firmly based on the Old Testament's conception of a vicarious and propitiatory sacrifice is, not more clearly but more extensively shown in the epistle to the Hebrews. It uses all the sacrificial language. Hebrews 2:17 has already been quoted with its verb *ilaskesthai.* But Hebrews only speaks more extensively, for all references to the blood of Christ carry the same message.[1]

Finally, Christ was the lamb of God. By his accepting the penalty of our sins, he satisfied the justice of God, thus propitiating God and reconciling God to those who had been his enemies, so that God could be both just and the justifier of him who had faith in Jesus.

---

1. Compare B.B. Warfield's devastating ridicule of liberalism's attempt to rid the New Testament of the ideas of expiation, reconciliation, and propitiation: *Biblical Doctrines,* Chapter nine, "Christ our Sacrifice," especially pp. 429ff.

14. Satisfaction

The paragraph just above said that Christ satisfied the justice of his Father. This demands special mention. From sub-apostolic times well into the Middle Ages the predominant view was that Christ's death was a ransom paid to Satan. Satan had certain rights over man, whom he had enslaved, and man could not be redeemed without someone's paying a satisfactory ransom-price to Satan. Bernard of Clairvaux, tremendously influential, the instigator of the bloody and disastrous second crusade, held this view in opposition to Abelard. He was not so much persuaded that Abelard's theory was wrong and another was right as he was that all theories were wrong and that theologians should not think. He condemned Abelard's influence that resulted in "boys in the street" discussing the doctrine of the Trinity. On the contrary, ecstasy is better than understanding and more is to be learned in trances and visions than by reasoning. He also defended the rapacity of the hierarchy. One of Abelard's students, Arnold of Brescia, agitated for the restoration to the people of the wealth the priests had extorted from them. Bernard had to acknowledge that Arnold was no libertine—he was an ascetic—but charged him with being in league with the devil, hungering and thirsting after the blood of souls. In spite of the fact that two of Abelard's publications were condemned by the Church, Protestants today are apt to rate him as a vigorous Romanist because of his strong insistence on the sacrifice of the mass.

Conservative theologians of the present century often describe Abelard's theory of the Atonement as the Moral Influence Theory. Abelard did indeed stress the idea that Christ's sacrifice stimulates our love and advancement in sanctification. But his theory is hardly the modern Moral Influence Theory such as is found in Horace Bushnell. Abelard held that Christ paid a ransom, not to Satan, but to the Father. He compares "the results of Adam's sins with those of Christ's obedience and makes use of the principle of merit."[1] He speaks of Christ's death as a sacrifice for sin and uses the expressions of I Peter that Christ bore our sins. The trouble is, of course, that Abelard, in spite of his great logical ability, was in this case neither complete nor consistent. He was also disliked, misunderstood, and was the target of many false accusations.[2]

Bréhier even considers Abelard to have been a Platonic realist, at least in theology (pp. 586, 591), though in philosophy he is clearly an Aristotelian.

Anselm (1109), somewhat Abelard's senior, had already renounced the theory that Christ's sacrifice was offered to Satan. He spoke of it as a satisfaction of the Father's honor. We who speak of satisfaction of the Father's *justice* may excuse Anselm on the ground that justice is a component of honor; and the prerogatives which Anselm assigns to honor can easily be transferred to justice; but it remains true that Anselm did not make the doctrine so precise as the Reformers did. Although Anselm's treatise *Cur Deus Homo* was a notable advance in the development of theology, it had at least two flaws, one merely peculiar, the other fatal. Peculiarly Anselm calculated the number of elect saints as equal to the number of fallen angels, so that the population of heaven would not be diminished by their exclusion.

The fatal flaw is that Anselm professed to obtain the doctrine of the Satisfaction without depending on Scripture. It may, it does, sound incredible that "leaving Christ out of view (as if nothing had been known of him) it [this book] proves, by

---

1. Robert S. Franks, *A History of the Doctrine of the Work of Christ*, (Hoddard and Stoughton, 1918), Vol. I, p. 190.

2. Emile Bréhier, *Histoire de la Philosophie*, 1951, Tome I, #3, p. 583.

absolute reasons, the impossibility that any man should be saved without him" (*Anselm*, tr. by S.N. Dean, Chicago, 1926, p. 177). This is from the *Preface*. The idea is repeated once or twice; and at the end the final remark of Boso, Anselm's pupil to whom he is talking throughout, is "I see the truth of all that is contained in the Old and New Testament, for . . . leaving out what was taken from the Bible . . . you convince both Jews and Pagans by the mere force of reason" (p. 287).

The first section of this treatise, with the subhead "Introduction on Method," stressed the indispensability of Scripture. All the more should it be stressed, because, as will become clear a bit later, Jonathan Edwards and A.A. Hodge, though admittedly they do not exclude Scripture so completely as Anselm, nonetheless derive some of their theses from experience.

That justice rather than honor is the more precise factor, Romans 3:25-26 makes unmistakably evident. One can say with considerable plausibility that Romans 3:21-26 is the most important paragraph in the Bible. Verse 25 says that God set forth Christ—the verb means *to design, to purpose*, or *to set forth publicly*—as a propitiation. The idea of propitiation has as its background the wrath of God, mentioned in Romans 1:18 and specified from that verse on to 3:20. In verse 21 Paul calls attention to God's righteousness. This righteousness has two forms, one which is in some way connected both with Jesus and with those who believe on him, but also in verse 25 the righteousness of God himself. Now the point of all this is that God so arranged Christ's death as a propitiation that God might be two seemingly incompatible things: that he might be not only the justifier of him who believes in Jesus, but also that he himself might be just in so doing.

Though this treatise is not a commentary on the Westminster Confession, nonetheless the Confession evidences the conclusions and beliefs of its authors and of their numerous adherents. One phrase in VIII, v, is "The Lord Jesus, by his perfect obedience and sacrifice of himself . . . hath fully satisfied the justice of his Father." In addition to Romans 3:25, 26 the footnote adds as supporting references, Romans 5:19, Hebrews 9:14, Ephesians 5:2. This is Calvinism; but it is also Lutheranism as well. The Augsburg Confession (1530) says briefly, "by his death hath satisfied for our sins" (Art. IV). The Formula of Concord, first written in German, then badly translated into Latin, and then somewhat amended and put into better Latin, though it stresses, as one might expect, justification by faith alone, is painfully deficient as to the work of Christ. Last century I.A. Dorner, a notable though not always the most orthodox of theologians, and for this reason more convincing, stated, "Contemplating humanity in Christ as making satisfaction to the divine Justice, God sees in him, who suffered for us, and in love to the divine Justice offered himself a sacrifice to God . . ." (*A System of Christian Doctrine*, tr. by Cave and Banks, Edinburgh, 1882; Vol. IV, p. 116).[1]

On the next page Dorner mentions the satisfaction of justice twice. Page 121 refers to "punitive justice;" the following page speaks of "guilt and actual penal desert" and "a satisfaction to the divine justice." This, I believe, is sufficient evidence of the historic Lutheran position.

It is clear therefore that the entire Protestant Reformation, namely its two branches, Lutheranism and Calvinism, agreed that Christ's death was a sacrifice to propitiate the wrath of God and to preserve his justice as he justified the sinner.

---

1. One evidence of Dorner's defection from strict Lutheran orthodoxy is the word *humanity* in this quotation. The Formula of Concord stresses the cooperation of both natures: "To overthrow both errors we unanimously believe, teach and confess that Christ is truly our righteousness, but yet neither according to the divine nature alone, nor according to the human nature alone . . ." (Article III, 1).

In expounding this doctrine and in defending it against non-biblical views the theologians, naturally, have used many arguments. These arguments, though elaborated with the best of intentions, have not always been without fault. Sometimes incomplete disjunctions have been used; important terms are often left undefined, or (though this is not a fault of the authors) if properly defined, they have become obsolete in modern language. The Christian public thereby remains confused and uninstructed. For example, earlier theologians would distinguish between distributive justice and governmental justice. H.B. Smith (*System of Christian Theology*, New York, 1884, pp. 464-470) distinguishes, or, better, fails to distinguish between distributive justice and general justice. He also refers to public justice: "The Atonement, while it indirectly satisfies Distributive Justice, does not consist in this: it consists in satisfying the Demands of Public Justice" (p. 470). A footnote to this sentence says, "Real, essential justice is what is meant by public justice." Clearly this is all very unclear.

Now some well-intentioned Christians may take offense both at this logomachy and its exposure. Justice is justice, they may say, and Christ satisfied God's justice, period! Yet for several reasons this distaste for clear thinking is unfortunate. First, it leaves a number of questions unanswered; it leaves the Biblical doctrine less explained than necessary. Second, at least two forms of justice must be distinguished, even if the distinction eventuates in headaches. Instead of some ancient terminology, let us speak of civil or financial justice as distinct from criminal justice. The distinction is this: If Mr. X owes Mr. Y a hundred dollars, financial justice is completely satisfied if Mr. Z pays the debt for Mr. X. But if Mr. X robs a bank or murders someone, Mr. Z cannot satisfy justice by taking his punishment. Criminal justice requires that the criminal himself, and no one else, must suffer the penalty. Now, since sin is a crime, not a financial debt, the satisfaction of divine justice without the penalty being imposed on the sinner himself constitutes a major problem. Then in the third place, a fallacious defense of a doctrine not only fails to establish the doctrine, but inclines many people to conclude that it is false. This conclusion of course is as fallacious as the theologian's blunder. If argument p does not prove that q is true, it by no means follows that q is false. But as illogicality is wide spread, a poor defense of the Atonement induces quite a few people to reject the doctrine. So far as is possible the theologian should try to prevent such a reaction: and the surest way to do so is to argue logically. For the next few paragraphs now, the attempt will be to explain and defend the conclusions, i.e., the Biblical doctrine of the Atonement, while exposing some of the fallacies used to support it.

The argument will become rather complex. Several problems are interwoven, so interwoven that first, second, and third becomes more of a mere numbering than of a logical progression.

First, if criminal justice requires the penalty to be executed on the criminal himself, how could God be satisfied with a substitute? Second, if God accepted the idea of a substitute, was it absolutely necessary that his Son should be that substitute? Was crucifixion and death, whoever the substitute might be, the only possible means? Could not God have been satisfied with some other penalty? Let us be clear on this. The Scripture teaches unmistakably that as a matter of fact Christ is the only substitute, that there is no salvation in any other name, and that it is necessary for us to depend on Christ's merits alone. This is how it actually is. But could God have chosen a different method? What he actually chose is obvious. What he might have chosen is a different question.

One impressive argument in favor of the cross is Christ's prayer, "Father, if it be possible, let this cup pass from me." The

implication is the impossibility of any other method. Nevertheless this prayer in itself shows only a necessity already
established. The process had already begun: God had made
some promises to Abraham, to David; and Christ had already
become incarnate. The process was far advanced. It was too
late to change it. So too with ourselves now. We can say that
belief in Christ is necessary to our salvation. So it is. This is the
actual condition. But none of this directly faces the question,
could God have chosen otherwise? The problem is that of the
absolute necessity of Christ's death.

Third, and this is implicated in point two, if God could not
have chosen otherwise, can we regard him as absolutely and in
every respect sovereign? If he be sovereign, could he not have
accepted, not merely a lesser penalty, but even no penalty at all?
This question requires us to state the relationship between
justice and sovereignty, and some theologians have done so in a
rather confusing manner.

That God's justice is somehow involved had already been
made clear. Romans 3:25-26 cannot be otherwise interpreted.
Justice is clearly one of God's attributes. The Shorter Cate-
chism, which every child should have memorized before
entering high school, says, "God is a Spirit, infinite, eternal, and
unchangeable in his . . . justice. . . ." It is strange that a very
orthodox theologian, like Arthur W. Pink, could write even a
small volume on *The Attributes of God* without mentioning
God's justice.[1] We shall do more than mention it.

---

1. A.W. Pink, in common with others, makes use of false disjunctions. On page 12 of
this volume he says, "nor is God known by the intellect. 'God is Spirit' (John 4:24), and
therefore can only be known spiritually." But *knowing* is *ipso facto* intellectual. "God is
just" is a proposition to be understood. No doubt sin hinders and even prevents a man
from knowing this truth; but if we are at all to know that God is just, we must use our
intellects, our minds, our understanding, for this is what knowledge is. One man's mind
may be "spiritual," *i.e.*, illumined by the Holy Spirit, and another man's mind not; but
whatever either of these men knows is known intellectually. When the Holy Spirit

Jonathan Edwards[1] stressed the justice of God, not only in his famous sermon, *Sinners in the Hands of an Angry God*, but also in his other sermons and discourses. But as A.A. Hodge says essentially the same things, in greater detail, it is necessary only to recommend Edwards to the contemporary public. John Murray, of recent date, writes in the same tradition, but more popularly and in less detail. Some of his material serves very nicely as a preparation for A.A. Hodge.

These men and others ordinarily say that there was no *necessity* for God to save anyone, but if he wanted to save someone, it was *necessary* for him to use the method of the cross. For example, "It should be understood that it was not necessary for God to redeem men. The purpose to redeem is of the free and sovereign exercise of his love. But having purposed [at some time or other?] to redeem, was the only alternative the blood-shedding of his own Son?" Then John Murray answers in the affirmative.[2] To defend this answer he adds these lines on the next two pages: "Those who think that in pursuance of God's saving purpose the cross was not intrinsically necessary are, in reality, not dealing with the hypothetical necessity of the atonement, but with a hypothetical salvation. For, on their own admission they are not saying that the *actual* salvation designed and bestowed could have been enjoyed without Christ, but only salvation of lesser character and glory."

What persons made this "their own admission" Murray does not say. It is tautological and otiose to insist that, had salvation been accomplished by a different method, the saints in heaven could have had no memory of Christ's being crucified. They

---

controls a man's thoughts, the thoughts are still thoughts. To repeat, knowing or understanding is *ipso facto* intellectual; and false disjunctions are to be rejected because they distort the message of the gospel.

1. *The Works of Jonathan Edwards*, Leeds and Philadelphia, 1811. Vols. VII, VIII.

2. *The Atonement*, Presbyterian and Reformed Publishing Company, 1962, p. 10.

would, nevertheless, be free from sin and would enjoy all beatific blessings. With the exception of the lack of memory of something that had not happened, the heavenly state would be the same. How can one know that this would be "salvation of lesser character and glory"?

His earlier book gives a somewhat more detailed exposition.[1] He notes that Augustine and Aquinas both spoke of "hypothetical necessity;" whereas most Protestants defend absolute necessity. The term "hypothetical necessity" means that there were other possible methods, but that God chose this one. Since God could have chosen another method, there is nothing in God's nature that makes the actual method of the cross indispensable. Murray's view is of course that salvation was not necessary—there was nothing in God's nature that made salvation necessary—but since he freely chose to save some, he could not possibly have chosen any other means.

Murray quotes a number of verses to support his position; but it seems to me that none of them proves his point. They all insist and make perfectly clear that God chose the method of the cross. They do not show that a different method was impossible. In addition to the Scriptural references Murray advances three arguments, each one a logical fallacy. He seems to sense that they are fallacious, for on page 13 he introduced them by saying, "In adducing these considerations it must be remembered that they are to be viewed in coordination and in their cumulative effect." But the cumulative effect of several fallacies is simply multiplied illogicality. Then on page 17 he argues that this absolute necessity is the only situation in which Christ's death can be the "supreme exhibition of love." But this is very doubtful. Some people might favor the exact contrary: If God chose the method of the cross without being necessitated

---

1. *Redemption Accomplished and Applied*, Eerdmans, 1955, pp. 11-17.

to do so, his love would have been more clearly, not less clearly, demonstrated.

One must be careful when reading the works of John Murray. He has a remarkable control of the English language, is in most cases quite orthodox, but is sometimes deficient in logic. In addition to the example just cited, his booklet *The Free Offer of the Gospel*[1] comes to a strange conclusion.

To prepare for the conclusion the booklet (p. 14), in speaking of Ezekiel 33:4-11 he says, " 'I have no pleasure in the death of the wicked'—admits of no limitation or qualification; it applies to the wicked who actually die in their iniquity." Whether this exegesis accords with the Westminster Confession III, 3, 7; V, 6; and XXXIII, 2 is not at present the point at issue; it is mentioned to prepare for the conclusion. On page 15 the booklet repeats, "It is absolutely and universally true that God does not delight in or desire the death of a wicked person." Still it is not clear how God could fore-ordain the death of a wicked person without desiring it. Then again, the booklet applies Ezekiel 33:11 to all mankind, whereas the text itself mentions only the house of Israel. In the case of Isaiah 45:22-23 Murray's interpretation implies universal salvation and not merely a universal offer. The mention of God as creator in Isaiah 45:12, 18 "has the effect of bringing to the forefront a relationship which he sustains to all men alike" (p. 20). Of course Murray and Stonehouse do not believe in universal salvation; but their language betrays their confusion: "While, on the one hand, he has not decretively willed that all be saved, yet he declares unequivocally that it is his will and, impliedly, his pleasure that all turn and be saved" (pp. 20-21). But if it was his pleasure that all be saved, how could Isaiah say, "He shall

---

1. Prepared with the cooperation of Ned B. Stonehouse and presented by them as a report to the General Assembly of the Orthodox Presbyterian Church in 1948; reprinted with slight corrections, no publisher, no date mentioned.

see of the travail of his soul and be satisfied"? Job 42:2 says, "No purpose of thine can be thwarted." And is not a purpose a desire? And does not God do all his will? In Psalm 135:6 God says, "Whatsoever the Lord pleased, that did he." Had he pleased to save everybody he would have saved them. He did not save them. Therefore he had not pleased to.

Now, it is interesting to see how Murray and Stonehouse try to manage the problem they have created. "God himself expresses an ardent desire for the fulfillment of certain things which he has not decreed. . . . This means that there is a will to the realization of what he has not decretively willed, a pleasure towards that which he has not been pleased to decree. This is indeed mysterious" (p. 26).

Now note what has happened. The two authors have used exegesis and argument in such a way as to produce a contradiction. But they are so sure of their arguments that they are unwilling to admit that they could have possibly made a mistake. This is not intellectual modesty. When one's thoughts lead one to contradiction, the logical and humble thing to do is to go back and find where the mistake occurred.[1]

Arguments are sometimes intricate, even when the topic is the Atonement. Indeed on this topic the arguments must become intricate, for the plan of salvation, in its entirety, covers innumerable details. Therefore prior to a resolution of the problem of justice versus sovereignty, the absolute or the hypothetical necessity of Christ's death, the exact meaning of *necessity* when referring to God and its relation to the *free* exercise of God's love, a discussion on federal headship, that of Adam and that of Christ, seems essential.

---

1. A briefer but better discussion of this one point is given by Gary D. Long, *Definite Atonement*, Presbyterian and Reformed Publishing Company, 1976, pp. 14-16. The remainder of the book also is excellent.

15. Federal Headship

The most important Biblical paragraph on federal headship is Romans 5:12-21; and the best exegesis is that of Charles Hodge in his tremendous *Commentary on the Epistle to the Romans*.[1] W.G.T. Shedd's commentary is also very good.

While waiting to obtain and study these commentaries, the reader may pass his time by wading through the next few shallow paragraphs here.

Romans 5:12-21 is obviously a comparison, of some sort, between Adam and Christ. Interesting, and surprising to us, is the fact that Paul expects his readers to know already what the function of Adam was and to learn by that what the function of Christ was. Today the explanation must be given in reverse. That Adam and Christ had similar relationships to certain groups of human beings is perfectly clear. The question is, what was that function? Since there is a similarity, any explanation that does not apply to both Adam and Christ must be wrong.

Pelagius, the opponent of the great Augustine, is proved wrong because Romans asserts and he denies that Adam's sin, not ours, is the cause of death. The analogy is further destroyed when Romans denies and Pelagius asserts that we gain eternal life by our own acts of righteousness. Then, also, Pelagius cannot explain why death, the penalty of sin, is more extensive than the range of voluntary transgressions—infants die before having voluntarily committed any transgression.

In opposition to a somewhat different view which makes death the result of inherent depravity, the verb *ēmarton* in Romans 3:23 and 5:12 does not mean "become corrupt." On the contrary, depravity is a part of death, not the cause of death.

---

1. Hodge's brilliance appears all the more clearly when contrasted with Dabney's attempt to refute him.

Likewise Romans denies that life results from infused righteousness. The ground of justification is no subjective state of
ours; the ground is Christ's finished work.

The reason or ground for our death and then for our
regeneration is the action of a substitute or representative.
Verses 17, 18, 19 stress *one* man. The act of one man caused our
death, including depravity; and the act of one man caused our
resurrection from death. Verses 13, 14 explain representation;
they do not explain imitation or depravity.

To sum up, Adam and Christ were our representatives.
They acted for us, instead of us; and what they did is attributed,
reckoned, or imputed to us. Those who were represented by
Adam, and this includes all human beings with one exception,
died by his act. Note above, *ēmarton* means *sinned*, not *became
corrupt*. It is aorist and thus refers to one past act, not to our
many present acts. Similarly those whom Christ represented—
his people, those God gave to him, the elect—live because he
crowned a sinless life with a substitutionary sacrifice, and rose
from the dead.

To speak of Adam as our representative is to identify him
as the *federal head* of the human race. The various difficulties
mentioned in the previous few paragraphs come to a head in
A.A. Hodge's[1] defense of federal headship.

First, though this will not be the crucial part of the
criticism, A.A. Hodge does not rely entirely on the Scriptures.
Part of his argument is based on the use of so-called natural
reason. Unlike Anselm he does not totally exclude the Scripture—far from it; but nonetheless he does not appeal to *Sola
Scriptura*. This appeal to natural reason leads him into some
peculiar argumentation.

---

1. *The Atonement*, Philadelphia, 1867.

Let us not suppose that Anselm and the two Hodges were the only ones who grounded their theology, partially at least, in the uninformed intellectual resources of sinful man. H.B. Smith, previously mentioned, did the same. He writes (*op. cit.*, p. 439), "This necessity [of a vicarious Atonement] may be argued on the grounds of man's moral nature: an atonement is eminently adapted to man's convictions and needs as a moral being." If, now, one assumes that man has such convictions, no doubt the vicarious atonement is eminently adapted to them. But adaptation is no proof that such an atonement is necessary. Perhaps other methods also could have been effective. Smith continues: "Man's conscience assures him of the supremacy, the absolute supremacy, of righteousness. . . . " But anyone who is familiar with Homeric religion would be inclined to disagree. Anyone familiar with Sodom and Gomorrah would likewise disagree. Smith of course could not have known of contemporary American abortionists, but he should have remembered the customs of pagan savages. Then some lines below he adds, "the necessity of an atonement is seen in the fact that it has actually been made. . . . An argument for the necessity of the atonement may also be derived from the general consent of mankind. . . . This universality proves [certain points] . . . according to *natural* conscience" (pp. 440-441).

Both parts of this quotation are unacceptable. First, the fact that Christ was actually crucified does not prove that it was eternally necessary. At least, it does not of itself prove such necessity. Perhaps with some additional premise it might do so. What such a premise might be, we shall discuss later. Then, second, the argument from general consent and natural conscience can in no way be made valid. Hume, Kant, Hegel, Russell, Dewey, the Logical Positivists, and many contemporary theologians entertain no such idea. Confucianism seems to have no such idea, and probably Shintoism has none either, though I am not sufficiently informed about it to say. At any rate, Smith can produce no evidence of any *universal* consensus. Empirical observation can never discover anything universal. Hence I claim that Smith's arguments on this point are logical fallacies based on unknowable premises. But now back to Hodge.

In chapter VII he describes Adam in his probationary state as being "as well endowed and circumstanced as any individual of his natural order . . . could possibly be" (p. 78). For this assertion he adduces no Scriptural support and presumably depends on the assumption that the "facts of the case are indubitably proved by the natural reason and universal experience of mankind" (p. 79). But would not natural reason more likely say that inability to sin, impossibility of punishment, and unalterable well-being would have been a better endowment and far better circumstances than the admittedly Biblical description of Adam's probation? Now, natural reason may be mistaken in this judgment, but that is all the more reason for not making this sort of reason the criterion by which one justifies the ways of God to man.

The reader will remember that earlier two types of justice were differentiated. Criminal justice will not impose the penalty on a substitute. But God does so; nor can we argue that sin is not a crime. Hodge indeed wishes to show that God is just in appointing Adam federal head of the race and in imputing the guilt of his sin to his posterity. Hodge is so anxious to emphasize justice that he says, "God, by a strictly judicial, *not sovereign* [italics mine], act justly imputes Adam's apostatizing act to us" (p. 112). This is a bold assertion of justice and a bolder denial of sovereignty. But he offers no reason for either one. He simply says, "this imputation . . . simply (a) recognizes our legal oneness with Adam and consequent common responsibility with him for the guilt of his public sin; (b) consequently charges the guilt of his sin to our account; and most righteously treats us according to the demerit of that sin" (112). But these sentences are not reasons or explanations: They are restatements of what needs to be explained. Undoubtedly the two doctrines are Biblical: the question is whether Hodge's defense of them is satisfactory.

He had previously said, "It is absolutely impossible for a devout mind to admit that God can be the immediate author of sin" (p. 81). This seemingly unexceptionable declaration is, however, defective on two counts. First, is it not at least possible, rather than impossible, that a more remote principal can be responsible for what he causes mediately through an agent? Second, theologians hardly ever define the phrase "author of sin." Until the meaning of these words is clarified, an argument in which they play so important a role cannot be evaluated. Arminius, a remarkable exception, defined it as "God sins and God alone sins." Is this what Hodge means? Even if Hodge does not mean that God alone sins, does he mean that God sins? What is sin? Is it defined by the law? To what law and to what authority is God subject? Can God dishonor his parents or commit adultery? Is it sin for God to cause a man to sin? If it be, what law did he break? On such an important subject as this, the key terms should be made as clear as possible.

Hodge does indeed say this much: "God cannot originally create agents with an inherent corrupt nature . . . for that would constitute him the author of sin" (p. 82). This, however, does not define the phrase. If one should say, "murder is sin," he is only giving an example of sin—he is not defining it. So also, to say that an original creation of corrupt natures would make God the author of sin is to give only an example, which is still subject to the question, Why? But there is something worse in that last quotation. If God could not have *originally*, in Genesis one and two, created depraved natures, can he later create men as

sinners without becoming the author of sin? If doing so in
Genesis is unthinkable, is doing so in Exodus permissible? The
point is that Hodge will later say that God has been continually
and immediately creating inherently corrupt souls for some
thousands of years. More of this later.

Hodge definitely wants to defend the justice of God. "God
will not inflict . . . evil upon any moral agent whose natural
claims as a dependent creature have not previously been justly
forfeited" (p. 82). This statement seems to have a hidden
presupposition. It seems to depend on the idea that a created
human being has natural claims that God must respect. But
does not this conflict with the Biblical figure of the potter and
the clay? This figure of speech occurs several times in the Bible.
Its point is that the Potter, if he does not like a pot, can smash it
and make another. Obviously a pot can have no claims over the
Potter. He can make one for honor and one for dishonor as he
pleases. This accords ill with the idea that a man has any natural
claims over God.

What then about a just forfeiture of such claims? A just
probation, according to Hodge, must "afford at least as much
opportunity of success as liability to failure" (p. 82). But since
Christ had been slain before the foundation of the world in
order to save sinners, Adam had no chance—there was no
possibility whatever—of avoiding sin. Yet Hodge continues,
"*On what ground of justice* (italics his) does God inflict this
terrible" penalty of sin?

16. Absolute Necessity

The Hodges of course were neither the first nor the last to
speak on this matter. Before them George Smeaton in his work
on *The Atonement according to Christ and his Apostles*, (Sover-

eign Grace edition, Grand Rapids, no date, perhaps between 1950 and 1970) has several sections on the necessity of the Atonement. He does not organize his work on systematic principles, but rather, as the title indicates, follows the method of Biblical Theology. His more than 500 pages, which are not numbered consecutively in this edition, are a rewarding examination of the Biblical material. Although he is more systematic than he probably realized, his Biblical method sometimes fails to make it clear whether he holds Christ's death to be absolutely necessary, or necessary only on the basis of the prior non-necessary divine decision to save some. Even when he uses the term *absolute*, his language does not make it quite clear which of the two ideas he supports. He seems to ignore, confuse, or mix them. But if he really mixes them, he must agree with absolute necessity in its strongest technical sense. He is, to be sure, quite clear on the absolute necessity that sin should be punished: "punitive justice . . . demands satisfaction for sin. It is as eternal and necessary as anything belonging to his self-existing nature. . . . He cannot but punish sin just as . . . he cannot lie" (p. 16). Granted: But is a gracious salvation equally necessary? Could God have refused to save anyone? Some of his sentences, at least if taken alone, cause us to wonder. For example, after quoting the verse, "So must the Son of Man be lifted up," and after emphasizing the word *must*, Smeaton adds, "the *must* indicating a necessity flowing from God's justice and from his decree, if men were to be saved" (p. 17). This sounds as if God was not "necessitated" to save anyone, but was necessitated to one method, if any were to be saved. Yet, it is not absolutely necessary to draw that conclusion. His following paragraph is also inconclusive. He is satisfied to say simply, "the atonement was necessary." The paragraph ends with ". . . the rectitude of God . . . presupposes . . . the necessary demand of an atonement" (p. 18).[1]

Yet there are hints that Smeaton disagreed with what the Hodges later said and asserts the absolute necessity of a redemption. Examining the words of Christ, as a Biblical theologian must do, in the subsection entitled "Separate Sayings which Affirm or Imply the Necessity of the Atonement," he exegetes as follows, of which I shall quote parts and summarize other parts.

"On several occasions the Lord refers to the necessity of his death, but often stops short at the fact that it had been foretold. Was there any deeper reason assigned by him? Yes: there are various allusions, direct and indirect, to a deep inner necessity for his atoning work" (p. 10). Smeaton then speaks disparagingly of some unnamed theologians who "regard the alleged necessity of the atonement in no other light than as a semi-philosophic theory." Though it is not exegetical as Smeaton wants his arguments to be, but is clearly "semi-philosophical," he makes a persuasive, though not strictly conclusive, point that "We cannot conceive of such a stupendous [event as the death of God's Son] if it were not necessary." This almost but perhaps not quite requires redemption to be absolutely necessary—not merely that if there were to be a redemption, Christ's death would be necessary on that hypothesis. The next sentence, however, seems to return to the hypothetical view: "There could be no other reason . . . for God . . . to suffer on the cross . . . if sin could have been remitted without satisfaction." Hence with these semi-philosophical arguments Smeaton's necessity seems to be based on a reason

---

1. In the Appendix, pp. 529-531, Smeaton talks about ABSOLUTE NECESSITY as being the view of both the Lutheran and the Reformed churches. But the context does not clearly rule out the possibility that God could have sovereignly decreed a different method of salvation. Yet he rejects the view that "Forgiveness of sins and justification of grace lies absolutely in the divine imputation; that is, in God's counting it enough."

deeper only than the necessity to fulfill prophecy. Moving closer to exegesis on the next page he adds, "The whole Old Testament system of sacrifices was calculated . . . to sharpen the conviction that sin required a higher sacrifice" than that of bulls and goats. That Smeaton does not have absolute *sovereignty* in mind is clear from his reference to "supreme justice" which must be satisfied "before salvation can be bestowed" (p. 13).

Defending the purpose of the Incarnation as redemption, so that the Logos would not have become flesh unless man had sinned, he states, "the Incarnation was . . . not necessary except on the supposition of redemption" (p. 19). Here he is opposing the view that some epistemological or ontological or revelatory function required an incarnation even if the race had remained perfectly righteous. So far so good. Then he adds, "This greatest work of God is still but a free work or deed, not necessary to the Divine felicity, and therefore on the same footing with creation or any other Divine act toward the universe" (p.19).

The reason, as I see it, why Smeaton does not have the more profound problem in mind is his aim to refute heterodox theologians who think that the infliction of a penalty is not "absolutely" necessary under the present circumstances. These theologians "conceive of God only as a source of goodness . . . but not as the sovereign Lord or moral Governor . . . and that when God does punish in any case, it is as a father, and not as a judge" (p. 14). Even here, where he uses the word *sovereign*, his words do not mean that the salvation of anyone is absolutely necessary. This analysis is not a disparagement of Smeaton. Any author who wants to be thorough selects a particular topic. From this central point he may spread out into a few adjacent areas; but he is not called upon to wander too far. He may be ignorant of some remote territories, or he may have detailed opinions on them; but he need not and usually should not mention them. Smeaton has chosen certain topics and his discussion of those topics is superior to that of many contemporary authors. Now for Hodge.

A.A. Hodge's repeated emphasis on justice, and his manner of doing so, almost immediately produces the impression that he is subordinating God to some superior law of justice, thus impugning God's sovereignty. This pinpoints the problem of absolute necessity.

Such an impression is supported by Hodge's later procedure. His early remarks on the Governmental Theory (pp. 58ff.) assert several times the *intrinsic* rightness of the moral law, an intrinsic rightness superior to the divine will: "He wills the precept *because* (italics his) it is intrinsically right." Hence there seems to be something superior to the will of God. But before quoting Calvin to the contrary, one may ask whether Hodge means only that God's will is subordinate to God's intellect, and that therefore there is no moral principle superior to God. Such a reply, however, entails a distinction between God's intellect and God's will, so that one "part" of God is subordinate to another part. This, combined with the separation of the divine attributes, raises difficulties with the simplicity of God's being. But we must proceed with the ultimacy of moral principles and the absolute necessity of one particular method of atonement.

In chapter XXI, where Hodge discusses the Governmental Theory more fully, which theory in his opinion does not properly evaluate morality, he says, "Vice must have, therefore, the *ultimate* reason of its attracting divine displeasure *in itself*" (p. 336). The italics are mine, but the words "in itself" certainly suggest that the distinction between virtue and vice does not depend on God's sovereign will, nor even on his intellect, but on the ultimate intrinsic properties of morality itself to which God must be *attracted*. This indeed implies the absolute necessity of the cross, but at much too expensive a price. We shall also see that in another place Hodge contrasts justice with sovereignty and prefers the former. Do not these words—ultimate, intrinsic, attract, in itself—presuppose a principle of virtue independent of and superior to God?

No Calvinist claims that Calvin was infallible, but we all hold him in high regard and we should not be ignorant of what he said on the subject. Beginning with the question of the necessity of the Atonement Calvin asserts, "If an inquiry be made concerning the necessity of this, it was not indeed a simple, or, as we commonly say, an absolute necessity, but such as arose from the heavenly decree" (*Institutes*, II, xii, 1). Contrary to Anselm (*Cur Deus Homo*, I, 12) namely, "When it is said that what God wishes is just, and that what he does not wish is unjust, we must not understand that if God wished anything improper it would be just, simply because he wished it," Calvin writes,

> . . . how exceedingly presumptuous it is only to inquire into the causes of the divine will, which is in fact and is justly entitled to be, the cause of everything that exists. . . . If you go further and ask why he so determined, you are in search of something greater and higher than the will of God, which can never be found (III, xxxiii, 2).

Then further, "Here they recur to the distinction between will and permission, and insist that God permits the destruction of the impious, but does not will it. But what reason shall we assign for his permitting it, but because of his will?" (III, xxiii, 8). There is no mistaking Calvin's meaning. "The will of God is the highest rule of justice." A moral principle is "just for this very reason, because he wills it." Calvin and Hodge bluntly contradict one another; and if Calvin was a Calvinist, apparently Hodge was not.

In chapter XVI Hodge makes some caustic criticisms, perhaps applicable to some phrases of some exponents of the

Governmental Theory. It is not my intention to say much about the Governmental Theory as such, but only insofar as it bases the method of atonement on the will of God. Incidentally Hodge acknowledges that Dr. Twisse, prolocutor of the Westminster Assembly, "and others, held it to be necessary simply because God had determined" so (pp. 53, 235). Against the great Westminster Calvinist as well as against the Governmentalists Hodge complains that "This theory is discredited by the fact that it is not developed in the first instance by a careful exposition and strict induction from Scripture. Its advocates do not pretend that they generate it out of Scripture; the most they claim is, that having developed it as a product of speculation, they are able to show that it *harmonizes* with all the facts of Scripture" (p. 341). Although Hodge uses the word *advocates*, in the plural, he seems to be referring chiefly to Barnes. Now, this complaint is a mixture of truth, possibly error, and at least innuendo.

It is true that Barnes, like Anselm, advances some thoughts "apart from any revelation" and insists that "we cannot think of him [God] otherwise than we do." With this notion, whether found in Anselm, Barnes, or whomever, I am in complete disagreement. But the *otherwise* includes Hodge himself, for he too has appealed to experience and universal consciousness.

Second, a quick reading of the quotation may give the impression that Barnes used no Scripture at all, or only a little, and that carelessly. Hodge apparently thinks that Barnes used only a little, carelessly. Out of 316 pages only thirty-nine appeal to Scripture. This may seem like a small proportion; but it is a greater proportion than is found in Hodge's book. At any rate, the proportion is not the main point. If thirty-nine pages of Scripture can be exegeted in the remainder of the 316, so as to confirm a view, the view would seem to be fairly well argued. Hodge has not shown that Barnes was careless in his handling of the Biblical material. Maybe he was, but Hodge gives no instances. Further, if Barnes can be opposed for using speculative arguments and natural reason, we must remember that Hodge uses experience also and does not base his conclusions solely on Scripture. Note that Hodge says, "If the question be asked *why* we ought to do right, no other answer can be given than that moral obligation in an ultimate fact of consciousness, having its own reason in itself, and from its very nature necessarily supreme" (p. 335). Is it not clear that Hodge has replaced Scripture with human experience, indeed with the experience of depraved human beings whose conclusions cannot be relied upon? Why cannot our position be that God has sovereignly imposed the Ten Commandments upon us? And in closer conjunction with the Atonement, why cannot justice be defined in terms of sovereignty rather than its being left undefined or sovereignty's being impugned? It seems to me quite wrong to say "Intelligence, moral and personal agency are inconceivable without *ultimate, unresolvable* principles of action and thought for which *no reason* can be given" (p. 336, italics mine). One must pause to ponder this astounding statement. Hodge is asserting that principles of morality are ultimate principles for which no reason can be given. Why, even Plato's World Of Ideas, his supreme principle, was a mind or person, as he says in the *Sophist*. But Hodge appeals to a non-personal principle for which no reason can be given. To this principle God himself is subject.

The topic of sovereignty, the choice of Adam as our federal head, the limitation of the Atonement to the elect as discussed in section 19 hereafter, and all this material on absolute necessity, results in stimulating an attempt by some people to absolve God of determinism and arbitrary action. In our own day, G.C. Berkouwer gradually abandoned Reformed theology, denied the inerrancy of Scripture, and accepted an existential or neo-orthodox subjectivism to save God from the obloquy of eternal decrees.

Basing his objections, not on Scriptural statements, but on his private estimate of the results of preaching predestination, he asserts that determinism makes consolation impossible and produces fear and uncertainty. Maybe it does with some people; with others it gives assurance of salvation. But to accept or reject any doctrine on the basis of the reception given to it is an anti-christian methodology. When Berkouwer also says that a determining God cannot be relied upon, and that such a view destroys the covenant, a logical mind would come to the opposite conclusion. But Berkouwer does not like logic. He further objects to a "speculative" doctrine which pictures God's sovereignty "abstractly." Theologians who use these two terms in such a connection usually give them no definition. If there be such things as abstract concepts (for I reject the Aristotelian theory of abstraction), but if there are such, would not *justification* and *sanctification* be examples? Are abstractions inimical to revelation? Is not the doctrine of propitiation abstract? Is not every doctrine? They were all abstracted from Scripture.

Berkouwer's procedure in deciding what to preach and what not to preach is to estimate the degree to which a topic will arouse faith in a hearer. Paul must have been very wrong in preaching the whole counsel of God, for much or at least some of the divine revelation arouses opposition instead. Furthermore, no preacher can arouse faith in an unbeliever. Faith is a gift from God. God chooses those to whom he will give this gift. This is certainly an arbitrary choice, in the sense that no qualities, characteristics, or accomplishments of the sinner induced God to choose him. Call it arbitrary or sovereign: In this case the two words mean the same thing, And surely it contributes more to comfort than to despair, in spite of

Berkouwer's contrary opinion.

Of course some people are assured of their salvation who ought not to be. The Roman church assures many. Others are assured that God is too good to punish anyone. But, as just said, the reactions of auditors is not the criterion for choosing a sermon topic; and in any case the fact that there are innumerable reactions to the same material makes such a choice impossible. The same sermon will be welcomed by one man on the right of the middle aisle and greatly irritate the lady on the left. Paul said, "Be ye imitators of me" (I Corinthians 4:16; 11:1), and he preached the whole counsel of God.[1]

To return for a final note to Hodge's attack on the Governmental Theory, he denies its accusation that the Biblical and orthodox theory implies the doctrine of limited atonement: "the true doctrine . . . does *not* [italics his] logically lead to any consequences which can be accurately expressed by the phrase *limited* [italics his] atonement" (p. 343). Incredible! But that is precisely what he says.

Ending these paragraphs on the Governmental Theory, and resuming the discussion of the justice of God in imputing guilt to Adam's posterity, we now proceed to the question "On what ground of justice does God inflict" not merely later punishment but particularly the "antenatal forfeiture" of the rights of newly created moral agents? Hodge classifies the answer under two methods. First, the subject may be discussed either on purely rationalistic principles, or on an interpretation of Scripture. Hodge should not only prefer this classification of the several views, but he should himself operate on purely rationalistic principles in conformity with his reliance on "the universal experience of mankind . . . as universally conceded."

---

1. For a masterful analysis of Berkouwer, compare *Berkouwer's Doctrine of Election*, Alvin L. Baker, Presbyterian and Reformed Publishing Company, 1981.

Actually he classifies the several views as either the affirmation or the denial of antenatal forfeiture. He asserts, what seems dubious, that these two methods amount to the same thing (pp. 83, 84).

There is no need to summarize Hodge's objections to Manichaeanism, for few such dualists remain today. But there are plenty who try to explain "*how* and *why* men always commence their conscious existence [as?] habitual sinners . . . by affirming the absolute self-determining power of the human will, and the consequent absolute 'impreventability of sin' " (p. 85).

Here Hodge's language is confusing, but his thought is clear. These people do not try to explain how and why men always commence their lives as sinners. The theologians referred to deny that babies commence as sinners. They are born, if not righteous, at least sinless. Then by free will they later choose to sin. Hodge perceptively notes that if this were so, one would expect at least a few to choose not to sin.

A different view does a little more justice to the universality of sin. The so-called New England Theology of Samuel Hopkins, the younger Edwards, and some others, though perhaps not popular in its precise original form, and by this time eclipsed by neo-orthodoxy, nevertheless has some descendants among the Arminian-minded groups. For example a Baptist friend of mine believed that children are sinless until they reach the age of ten or twelve, then they sin, and then they need to be saved. Though the earlier form of this view seems to have based universal sin on the sovereignty of God—an idea Hodge detested and condemns as pantheism, which it is not, or "virtual pantheism" (p. 89) a phrase whose meaning is unclear—the later form of the theory explains universal sinfulness as an inheritance of the parents' inherited corruption. This corruption is not a *penal* consequence of Adam's sin, but a result of the

natural laws of reproduction. In this view federal headship, with
its difficulties relative to substitution in criminal cases, has no
standing. Children are guilty of their own voluntary transgressions, not of Adam's.[1]

Another view which Hodge, not so justly, condemns is that
of W.G.T. Shedd. It may be called Platonic Realism. Hodge
describes it as asserting that "every individual member [of the
human race, Christ excepted] was *physically numerically* one
with" Adam. Now, if this is what Shedd said or thought, Hodge
could very legitimately call it nonsense. Adam, Moses, and Paul
are not numerically the same physical person. But can we
suppose that Shedd, who was at least moderately intelligent,
said or thought so? Though Hodge does not cite the pages, he
seems to be referring to Shedd's *Dogmatic Theology*, Vol. II, pp.
30ff. The passage begins with the words, "The doctrine of the
specific unity of Adam and his posterity removes the great
difficulties . . . that arise from the injustice of punishing a
person for a sin in which he had no kind of participation." The
next page says, "Adam and his posterity were specifically one in
the apostasy." This *specific* unity is mentioned a second time on
the same page. On page 32 he complains that "Edwards
supposes a unity of *individual* [italics his] persons aggregated
together instead of a simple specific nature not yet individual-
ized by propagation as in Augustinianism." In these pages, note
the repetition of *specific* unity.

Now if Shedd had never mentioned numerical unity at all,
Hodge would not have written as he did. Shedd does indeed
refer to a numerical unity and, because of the history of realism
and empirical nominalism, the language seems strange. On
page 35 Shedd says, "Augustine affirms . . . both a *specific* and

---

1. An interested student should read an account of Placaeus and the French National
Synod at Charenton, December 1644-January 1645.

numerical [italics his] unity . . . . Specific unity is of course the unity of a species . . . . A numerical may, or may not be a specific unity." This last phrase is strange because it is so unplatonic. Plato kept the Ideas or species quite distinct from the individual sensory objects, so that we do not expect anyone to say that a specific unity may be a numerical unity. But Shedd says it. To continue:

> In the instance of man the unity is both numerical and specific. The human nature while in Adam is both numerically and specifically one. But when it is subdivided and individualized by propagation, it is no longer numerically one. The numerically one human nature becomes a multitude of individual persons, who are no longer the single numerical unity which they were at first. But they are still specifically one.

I must confess that I feel some sympathy for Hodge as he rejects Shedd; but I also hold that he has misunderstood Shedd's position, which Shedd himself has inexcusably confused.

Shedd began by stressing specific unity. Like a good Augustinian he sharply distinguishes between species and individuals. "A specific unity," he says, "implies the possibility of the *division* of the one numerical substance among the propagated individuals of the species." But the latter half of this sentence is not good Augustinianism. The specific unity is never so divided that a part of it goes to one individual and another part of it to another individual. If this were so, as Plato made clear, no individual would be a man: He would be only part of a man. The species or Idea must be found entire, not divided, in every individual of the species. Now, it seems to me that, no matter how much Shedd oscillated, he meant, when speaking of the *numerical* unity of the species, simply that the species rose is one species and the species man is a second species. We cannot attribute to Shedd the utter stupidity of having said or thought that Moses and David were numerically the same individual.

Shedd intends his theory to alleviate the difficulty most people have with the notion that a remote grandchild must be punished for the sin of his distant ancestor. Perhaps it does, perhaps not. In any case, so it seems to me, we are not obliged to satisfy "the profound convictions of the human conscience" (p. 36). Representation can rest on divine sovereignty alone, and really must, for the so-called profound convictions are those of a race whose every member has a mind distorted by sin. But though Augustinianism does not by this justify the ways of God to man, it indeed helps one to understand what those ways are.

17. Traducianism

The various theological doctrines are so interwoven that it is sometimes difficult to know in what order to discuss them. As a professor once said of a work on philosophy, and no doubt of all works on philosophy, so also with theology one cannot understand the first chapter until after he has understood the last chapter. Shedd had prepared for the subjects just discussed in our previous section by a long passage on the origin of individual souls. He put it in his chapter on *Creation*. Hodge might well have done so, for he holds to the immediate creation of every soul at the moment of conception. But Shedd holds that the souls of the children are as much derived from their parents as their bodies are. The plan of the present treatise is to connect the origin of souls with federal headship and the imputation of guilt from Adam. The origin of souls was mentioned in that section, but its discussion was deferred.

Hodge, I mean A.A. Hodge, is, though both Hodges are, creationists. They both teach that each successive human soul is immediately created by God in billions of cases, billions of separate acts of creation. But his defense of this position and his arguments against traducianism are both beset with difficulties. In the first place he acknowledges (*op. cit.*, p. 111) that "without going the length of Realism, it appears probable that the divinely ordained representative . . . is conditioned on the generic unity of men as constituting a race propagated by generation." Note the term *propagated*. This means that traducianism is at least plausible. But Hodge does not want to go "the length of Realism." But if not, then what? Everyone who has had an introductory course in philosophy knows, or should know, that Aristotle and John Locke proposed an empirical method by which sensory observation could be transmuted into abstract concepts, which in turn form the basis for universal propositions. But Aristotle never spelled out the method; he depended on an illustration of an army in rout. Locke was more specific, but Berkeley demolished his argument. Hence the more philosophical readers may here wish to consider whether the generic unity Hodge suggests can be produced without adopting the realism he detests. As for Christ himself, though traducianism, operating through Mary alone, can account for his human soul, his federal headship cannot be accounted for, either by creationism or by traducianism. Not by creationism because even if his human soul had been a special creation, it is the Person and not just the human nature that is the federal head. Not by traducianism because Christ had no descendants. But this is not the case with Adam.

One reason why A.A. Hodge makes such a poor case for creationism is his imperious urge to refute realism. Thus he says, "The doctrine that each soul is severally and immediately created by God at the instant of conception[1] is obviously and

---

1. Note well that these words absolve from the charge of misrepresentation everyone who reports that creationism teaches the *immediate* creation of each and every soul.

absolutely inconsistent with the realistic view of human nature.
No Creationist can be a Realist" (p. 102). I am not sure that this
emphatic statement is altogether correct. For one thing, it may be
possible for a creationist and a realist to agree on the constitution
of human nature without agreeing on the immediate origin of
each soul. Nor is it true that every realist agrees with Plato. Shedd
certainly believed that God created the world and he did not
believe in the preexistence of souls; whereas Plato had no place
for any strictly creative Deity. After all, Augustine was a realist
and he argued strongly against Plotinus in favor of creation.

Since Hodge is so strongly opposed to realism, one may
oppose Hodge on that basis. For example, the theory of
imagination by which Aristotle aimed to produce concepts
which in turn would make universal judgments possible is open
to devastating attack.[1] Then if Aristotelian conceptualism be
rejected, only realism and nominalism remain; and the latter
must reduce the Trinity to tritheism or atheism. But the more
immediate rebuttal, and the one more appropriate to the present
treatise, is the Scriptural material.

Hodge seems to think that traducianism is inconsistent
with the federal headship of Adam: "Calvin . . . [et al.] unite in
affirming that we were in Adam representatively; that we really
and truly sinned in him because his sin is our sin, really and truly
our sin as to its federal responsibility" (p. 103). But far from
denying federal headship, traducianism offers a possible, even a
probable explanation of why God chose Adam to be our federal
head. Creationism allows only a physical or corporeal, not a
spiritual, connection between us and Adam.

Yet Hodge wants "hereditary corruption" (p. 104). But
how can corruption be hereditary if every new soul is an

---

1. Compare my *Three Types of Religious Philosophy*, The Craig Press, 1973; chapter III.
See also several other of my books.

immediate creation? Hodge surely does not help himself by his incomplete disjunctions. On two successive pages (103, 104) he argues "these men [Calvin, Beza, Turretin] were not Realists . . . they specifically explain . . . that we were in Adam *representatively*." Hodge's disguised premises are (1) that federal representation is impossible in realism, and (2) that Adam's being our representative cannot be harmonized with traducianism. These two premises are clearly untrue, for traducianism not only aims at but succeeds in making representationism more easily understandable. The two do not form an exclusive disjunction as Hodge maintains.

Another poor argument shortly appears. "If the entire genus was in Adam, the entire antediluvian race was, in the same sense, in Noah. If we were guilty co-agents in the first sin of the one . . . we must be . . . guilty of every one of the sins of Noah" (p. 106). This paragraph teems with confusion. First, we are indeed descendants of Noah. Second, the entire genus was in Noah, and is in us too. Otherwise we would not be human beings. As Plato so clearly said in his *Parmenides*, the Idea, or genus, is not like a canopy or tent in which each man is directly under only a part of the covering. The Idea or definition must be complete in every individual case, or in better Platonic language, every man must participate in the whole Idea.

But this in no way implies that we are guilty of any—let alone every one—of the sins of Noah. In fact we are not guilty even of Adam's sins, that is, his second, third, and fourth sin. We are guilty only of his first sin. Just because the federal head of the whole human race must be, or most appropriately is, its ancestor, it by no means follows that every ancestor must be a federal head. Hodge's logic is bad, very bad. Actually he is applying simple conversion to a universal affirmative. The point is that God chose Adam as federal head of the race; he did not so choose Noah. Had he chosen Noah and not Adam, then the antediluvians would not have been guilty of Adam's sin. Traducianism is a plausible explanation of federal headship, but it does not require two or more federal heads to make the race guilty.

Hodge's failure to refute traducianism and realism, does not *prove* that these two theories are true. There may be better objections than those Hodge has made. I do not happen to know any.

However, one's decision must be based on Scripture. And there are indeed Scriptural passages which, to put it modestly, seem to favor Shedd rather than Hodge.

Shedd divides his argument for traducianism into three parts: (1) Scripture, (2) Systematic Theology, (3) Physiology. The third part may be interesting, but it is useless. The first and second parts are the same thing. The second simply organizes the first. Therefore Shedd and the present treatise base the case on Scripture.

Shedd begins, "the Bible teaches that man is a species, and the idea [or definition] of a species implies the propagation of the entire individual out of it" (Vol. II, p. 19). This was what was meant a page ago in the reference to a covering tent in Plato's *Parmenides*. That the human race is a species, Shedd defends by the use of the term *man* in Genesis 1:26, 27. Note that God said, "Let us make man in our image and let *them* have dominion . . . male and female created he them." *Man* or *Adam* did not become a proper masculine noun until Genesis 2:19. Note too that Genesis 46:26 speaks of "the souls that came with Jacob into Egypt, which came out of his loins." Shedd also quotes a half a dozen verses from the New Testament. When Eve was taken from Adam's side, there is no mention of the creation of a second soul. Eve totally came out of Adam (I Corinthians 11:8). This supports the view that any child of Adam and Eve was born totally a member of the species. The entire person, not just his body, is propagated.

One may object that the new soul was immediately created, but that its creation is just not mentioned. Reply: Doctrines should not be based on silence.

It is not my desire to summarize Shedd's fifty or sixty pages of Scriptural argument. His work is easily obtainable and the student is urged to study it. However, whether found in Shedd or elsewhere, more Scriptural references than two or three in Genesis are needed.

That the propagation of the race is only corporeal, and not spiritual or mental also, that only the child's body and not his soul comes from the parents, seems to be denied in John 3:6: "That which is born of the flesh is flesh, and that which is born of the spirit is spirit." The Greek verb, occuring twice in this verse, and five times in the context, is *gennaō*, begat. It is the same verb that one finds in Matthew 1:1-16. In John 3:6 Christ is speaking to Nicodemus and "that which is born of flesh" is Nicodemus' unregenerated soul rather than his physical body. The verb indicates that Nicodemus received his unregenerated soul from his parents. This prevents the interpretation that *sarx* always refer to a sinful soul: To return to John again, 1:14 says that the Word was made flesh (*sarx*). Consider: The Word did not merely take to himself a physical body; he also took a reasonable or rational soul. He got them both through Mary. Similarly *sarx* in John 17:2 does not mean the body, certainly not the body alone, but rather Jesus gives eternal life to souls. *Sarx* sometimes means man's depraved nature; but this only enforces the point that it means the soul. A body cannot sin. Therefore the soul of Nicodemus came from his parents.

John 1:14 has already been mentioned, but one should also notice that the preceding verse denies that spiritual birth depends on heredity ("not of bloods"); but though natural birth is not explicitly mentioned, the verse implies that natural birth does so depend. Hence both soul and body come from parents. The soul, as well as the body, is born (compare again, 3:6).

Acts 17:26 does not say that God hath made of one blood all nations with respect to their bodies alone. The following verse, with its phrase "seek the Lord," clearly includes a man's mind or soul. Shedd and others cite other verses which interested students can search out. The accumulation of verses is important because some creationists give the impression that traducianism has only a few verses in its favor,[1] whereas the number is considerable.

The most important argument for traducianism is based on Genesis 2:2, 3. "God rested from all his work." "In six days God made heaven and earth . . . and rested on the seventh day" (Exodus 20:11). "God rested from *all* his works (*apo pantōn tōn ergōn*)" (Hebrews 4:4).

Perhaps the reader will permit a paragraph on Charles Hodge also. In his *Systematic Theology*, Vol. II, pp. 68ff. he discusses traducianism and creationism. Most of the section on the former depends on the alleged silence of Scripture on the subject: The various passages that traducianists use, he claims, are inconclusive. He even asserts that "The more enlightened and candid advocates of traducianism admit that the Scriptures are silent on the subject" (p. 68). This means, of course, that Shedd, who used Scripture passages, was either not enlightened or not candid. Hodge understands the word *flesh*, in those passages already cited, to mean precisely the body in contrast with the soul. Then when he comes to the transmission of inborn depravity, and the difficulty of thinking that God immediately creates sinful souls, he appeals to secondary and mediate causes, thus abandoning the idea of immediate creation: "We

---

1. Louis Berkhof, *Systematic Theology*, p. 200, "The few scriptural passages . . ., no clear teaching of scripture. . . ." At least Berkhof is honest enough to apply these remarks to both views.

do not know how the agency of God is connected with the operation of second causes, how far that agency is mediate, and how far it is immediate" (p. 69). Certainly this is a surrender of creationism. Traducianists are willing to say that the souls of men are "created" mediately, *i.e.*, by the mediation of parents, just as we may also speak of trees and animals as created objects. But these created objects on my front lawn were mediately created through the seeds or slips from earlier plants.

Charles Hodge at this point refers to his later chapter on original sin as a more explicit defense of creationism and the difficulty with God's immediate creation of sinful souls. This reference I take to be pp. 222ff., and perhaps also page 253. But none of this relieves him of his duplicity. On the latter page he allows that "It is moreover a historical fact universally admitted, that character, within certain limits, is transmissible from parents to children. Every nation, separate tribe, and even every extended family of men, has its physical, mental, social, and moral peculiarities which are propagated from generation to generation. . . . " But if God *immediately* creates the soul of the child, no mental or moral characteristics can be *propagated*.

The earlier section is equally unsatisfactory. His subhead was "Realism No Solution of the Problem of Original Sin." The main deficiency in his argument is that traducianism, as a theory of the origin of the soul, never claims to explain original sin. It is a view of the origin of the souls of Adam and Eve's descendants. Beyond that it may add that the derivation of the children's souls from their parents ties in nicely with God's choice of Adam as their federal head. This would have been so even if Adam had not sinned. But while traducianism and original sin are related, for all doctrines are in some way related in one system, the latter must receive its own explanation. Or, as

another example, the Atonement as such is not an explanation
of our sanctification. Nor do the sacraments explain our
resurrection at Christ's return. Hence Hodge's attempt to refute
traducianism, or realism, on the ground that it does not solve the
problem of original sin, is worthless.

All the less do these pages (222ff.) refute traducianism.
The main reason is that Hodge is violently opposed to realism.
In fact his argument against realism begins two pages back. A
few paragraphs ago I urged several objections against Hodge's
arguments. Maybe one more is allowable and sufficient:

> Realism . . . subverts the doctrine of the Trinity in so far
> that it makes the Father, Son, and Spirit one God only in the
> sense in which all men are one man. The persons of the Trinity
> are one God because they are one in essence or substance; and
> all men are one because they are one in essence. The answers
> which Trinitarian realists give to this objection are unsatisfacto-
> ry because they assume the divisibility and consequently the
> materiality of Spirit.

This quotation consists of three sentences. The first
sentence is doubtful. Hodge does not cite any author. Naturally
the Persons of the Trinity are one in the sense that all men are
one, and all horses; but it does not follow that the three Persons
are one only in that sense. For example, three human beings
have three wills; but the three Persons have but one will. Hence
the diversification of human beings is not identical to the
diversification of the Persons, for which reason we cannot
assert that the two unities are completely identical. The second
sentence seems to me to be quite true and therefore no
objection. Sentence three takes it as an objection and offers an
alleged reply. Realists, says Hodge, assume the divisibility of
essence and the materiality of Spirit. Hodge capitalizes the *S*.
Now if pagan Plato was worse than Christian realists, he must

have all the more asserted the divisibility of the essence. Actually he ridiculed it. Did Hodge never read Plato's *Parmenides*? And to suppose that Christian traducianists or Christian realists teach the materiality of Spirit, either the Holy Spirit or the human spirit, is ridiculous. Traducianists are traducianists because they believe that not only are the children's bodies derived from their parents' bodies, but also that their immaterial souls are equally derived from their parents' immaterial souls.

Kind reader, permit me to add a personal remark. I consider Charles Hodge by far the best of all American theologians. But his Scottish common sense *philosophy* was fortified with too much usquebaugh before he imbibed it.

J. Oliver Buswell, Jr. defends creationism in a most unfortunate way. In his *A Systematic Theology of the Christian Religion* (Zondervan, 1962, Vol. I, pp. 250-252) he speaks three times of Christ having been born with a sinless body: "The body of Christ was perfectly sinless." Nothing is said about a sinless soul. This is peculiarly strange, for, contrary to orthodox doctrine, Buswell teaches that "He, that is, his personal eternal being, his soul, became a human person, a human soul, without in any way ceasing to be a divine person, a divine Soul" (p. 251). But this is Nestorianism unless Buswell means to annihilate the divine Person; and other creationists would not be pleased with this defense of their doctrine.

This section will now conclude with a review of the objections raised against traducianism by Louis Berkhof (*Systematic Theology*, pp. 197-201).

Berkhof begins with a short but very fair statement of traducianism, including some of its Scriptural support. He refers to only one verse in favor of creationism, namely, Psalm 104:30. But if this verse teaches creationism, it follows that the souls of all animals and all plants are also immediately created.

Now, it is true that the Old Testament assigns both souls and spirits to animals, and if a creationist wishes to accept the point, he is consistent. Those who oppose the theory of traducianism in the case of human beings, but assert it of animals, are inconsistent. An interesting, if inconclusive point. But it certainly keeps God busy creating.

Berkhof's first objection is only half an objection. He begins by appealing to the simplicity and indivisibility of the soul, and concludes that the souls of the parents cannot divide to make a new soul. He offers no Scriptural support for this; and, as previously noted, the soul of Eve seems to be a contrary example. The second part of the first objection is a question: Does the new soul originate from the father or from the mother, or from both? Medieval theologians, as I have heard, held that the body comes from the mother and the soul from the father. That it comes from both is more plausible. Eve's soul was surely a special case; Christ's human soul could have come only from Mary. This was also a special, miraculous case. But inability to answer this question is no refutation of traducianism, especially if Scripture favors the fact.

Berkhof presses this question in his second objection by asserting that if the new soul is potentially in the souls of the parents, traducianism must be a form of materialism. This is utter nonsense. He also adds that it would make the parents *creators*. But since he cannot deny that the bodies of babies come from their parents, he must, if consistent, acknowledge that parents are indeed *creators* of bodies. It is strange how a truly intelligent theologian can be so irrational. The third objection is not an objection at all: It is something that traducianists admit, indeed assert, and use as an objection against creationism. Berkhof says, "(3) It proceeds on the assumption that, after the original creation, God works only mediately" (p. 198). This, however, is not precisely an assumption: It is an exegesis of Scripture.

Berkhof also argues that God in regeneration does not act mediately but immediately creates a new soul. Now, it is true that the apostle speaks about a new man and even a "new creature" (II Corinthians 5:17; Galatians 6:15). But if the Greek word in these two verses be understood as *bara* is used in Genesis, there would have come into being, *ex nihilo*, another person. One must remember that *regeneration*, in the epistles, is usually called a *resurrection*. Resurrection allows the individual sinner to remain himself. Well, *re*-generation does so too. Creation *ex nihilo* produces someone else.

The fourth objection is one that has become all too familiar with us through the Hodges. Traducianism is realism, and realism is bad. Without repeating the philosophic arguments about species, universal propositions, and non-existent images, we deny, on the basis of arguments already given, that traducianism "fails to give a satisfactory answer to the question why men are held responsible only for the first sin of Adam, and not for his later sins, nor for the sins of the rest of their forebears." This matter will appear again in the discussion on sovereignty.

Berkhof's fifth and last objection is equally faulty. Briefly it is that traducianism would result in Christ's having a depraved human soul. But this assumes that Adam was Christ's representative and federal head. This, however, is not the case, and the Westminster Confession explicitly rules it out: " . . . the guilt of this sin was imputed, and the same death in sin and corrupted nature conveyed to all their posterity descending from them *by ordinary generation*" (VI, 3). Incidentally, the verb *conveyed* suggests traducianism. The birth of Christ was miraculous and is not to be subsumed under the otherwise universal rule.

Berkhof then argues for creationism, first on an exegetical basis. Ecclesiastes 12:7, "Then shall the dust return to the earth as it was, and the spirit shall return to God who gave it," indicates "different origins" for soul and body. This is not surprising: Genesis 2:7 says so. But neither verse specifies the mode of propagation. God immediately formed earth into a body for Adam; does that mean that God immediately does the same for every individual? How Isaiah 42:5 fits into Berkhof's theory is difficult to say. Zechariah 12:1 says that God "formeth the spirit of man within him." But Amos 4:13, with the same Hebrew verb, says that God "formed the mountains also; and createth the wind." Does God immediately create every wind that blows down from Canada to chill us each winter? Did not God form a mountain in a Mexican cornfield a few years ago? It took him about a year to do it. Hebrews 12:9, which Berkhof next cites, speaks of God as "the Father of spirits." How can one get creationism out of this? He quotes "Delitzsch, though a traducianist [as saying] 'There can hardly be a more classical proof text for creationism.' " One cannot but wonder whether Delitzsch was speaking sarcastically, for if this is the best text creationists can find, traducianists need have no fear. In ancient Jewish society, and sometimes in American English, the term *father* does not mean a boy's immediate parent. Abraham Lincoln said, "Four score and seven years ago, our fathers. . . ." The Jews regularly referred to Abraham as their father (John 8:39). If the verse has any reference at all to the origin of souls, it suggests traducianism, not creationism. Berkhof really gives his case away by adding to the verse in Hebrews 12:9, Numbers 16:22, which says merely that God is the God of the spirits of all flesh. Well, of course; God is the God of all the universe.

The second argument is the philosophical point that while creationism recognizes "the immaterial and spiritual and therefore indivisible nature of the soul of man . . . the traducian theory on the other hand posits a derivation of essence, which, as is generally admitted, necessarily implies separation or division of essence." This is a misunderstanding of realism, one which the *Parmenides* ridiculed. Perhaps Berkhof is thinking of Tertullian. But Tertullian, though a Christian, and an important person in the development of the doctrine of the Trinity, was, strangely enough, a materialist. Very few Christians have been materialists. The next one I can think of was Thomas Hobbes in the seventeenth century. More recently behaviorism has been making headway in Christian colleges; but clearly this is not Christianity. At any rate Shedd and others were not materialists.

The third and last argument concerns Christology and argues that traducianism must make Jesus guilty of Adam's first sin. This was refuted earlier, and some elucidation will follow in the next section.[1]

18. The Sovereignty of God

Many of the matters discussed in the earlier sections—the Covenants, the Incarnation, the Satisfaction, and indeed Absolute Necessity—come to a head under the rubric of sovereignty. One question previously raised was whether God could have

---

1. In spite of the life and death seriousness of the doctrine of the Atonement, a seriousness which on one occasion forced Peter to cry out, Depart from me, for I am a sinful man, and by which the more conscientious person is affected more than the less conscientious, some unintentional humor occasionally relieves the tension. In a sermon before the London Baptist Congress, from which he quotes in his *Systematic Theology* (Vol. II, pp. 673-674), A.H. Strong, combining a defense of the true human nature of Christ with some reference to his federal headship, wrote: "Jesus . . . is the representative of all humanity. Consider for a moment what is implied in your being a man. How many parents had you? You answer, Two. How many grandparents? You answer, Four. How many great grandparents? Eight. How many great-great grandparents? Sixteen. So the number of ancestors increases as you go further back, and if you take in only twenty generations, you will have to reckon yourself as the outcome of more than a million progenitors." If so, may I add that if you take it back to Noah your ancestors, not in aggregate, but in that generation, will be several billion; whereas as a matter of fact they are exactly eight. Two at the time of Adam.

sovereignly dispensed with justice. The two Hodges decide in favor of justice and reject sovereignty. Let the reader understand that this treatise maintains that Christ satisfied the justice of his Father. What the treatise aims to show is that the Hodges and others have formulated an incorrect disjunction between the two. Or, to anticipate, justice is itself based on sovereignty. This includes the idea that the Atonement was absolutely necessary. The theology of Charles Hodge is impeccable on nearly every point, yet some of his paragraphs (as I have indicated in other publications) suffer from confusion.

The question, "How is justice related to sovereignty?" can arise only within the sphere of Calvinism. Lutheran theology is more anthropocentric than theocentric. Krauth, an influential Lutheran theologian, in his *The Conservative Reformation and its Theology* (pp. 123ff.), claims that Arminius was largely influenced by Lutheranism. Krauth's decisive example is Arminius' choice and denial of the five points of Calvinism: It was Arminius, not some Calvinist, who selected the TULIP as the essence of Calvinism. On this, says Krauth, Arminianism and Lutheranism are in accord. Some semi-calvinists are in partial agreement. A.H. Strong (*Systematic Theology*, II, p. 635) remarks, "We prefer to attribute God's dealings to justice, rather than to sovereignty." This statement is immediately connected with the imputation of Adam's guilt to his posterity, but it is reasonable to suppose that Strong would say the same thing of the Atonement also. The statement is vague, suggesting a mere preference that would allow some role to sovereignty if one should press it. Strong supports his preference by five considerations. The first is, "A probation [in the case of Adam] is more consistent with divine justice than a separate probation of each individual. . . ." If we end the sentence here, the reply is that most people would insist that a probation of each individual is more just, while imputation more clearly depends on sovereignty. Actually the sentence continues "of each individual with [his] inexperience, inborn depravity, and evil example, all favorable to a decision against God." But with the exception of the evil example, the conditions falsify the situation. Adam was equally inexperienced, and a probation for each individual could only occur if each were innocent as Adam was. That is, the theory rejects inborn depravity. Hence, the argument fails on two counts. Second, "A constitution which made a common fall possible may have been indispensable to any provision of a common salvation." The answer is, "may have been" is insufficient. To prove his point, Strong should have said "must have been." Perhaps it is wise to omit Strong's other reasons. They all seem irrelevant to me, but the reader can read Strong for himself and decide.

However, as was just said, the problem is essentially a problem for Calvinism because, unlike the other theologies, it stresses both justice and sovereignty. The question is, How are they related?

On this subject Charles Hodge has a peculiar paragraph. It seems to contradict itself. The subhead (*Systematic Theology*, I, p. 539) is "The Decrees of God are Free;" and the following quotation is a part of it:

They [the decrees] are rational determinations, founded on sufficient reasons. This is opposed to the doctrine of necessity, which assumes that God acts by a mere necessity of nature, and that all that occurs is due to the law of development or of self-manifestation of the divine being. This reduces God to a mere *natura naturans*, or *vis formativa*, which acts without design. The true doctrine is opposed also to the idea that the only cause of events is an intellectual force analogous to the instincts of irrational animals. The acts performed under the guidance of instinct are not free acts, for liberty is a *libentia rationalis*, spontaneity determined by reason. It is therefore involved in the idea of God as a rational and personal being that his decrees are free. He was free to create or not to create . . . to act or not to act . . . not from any blind necessity, but according to the counsel of his own will.

This paragraph contains considerable confusion; but before examining it, it will help to quote parts of the next paragraph in which Hodge more clearly shows his basic orthodoxy.

The decrees of God are free in the sense of being absolute or sovereign. . . . the decrees of God are in no case conditional. The event decreed is suspended on a condition, but the purpose of God is not. It is inconsistent with the nature of God to assume suspense or indecision on his part. If he has not absolutely determined on what is to occur, but waits until an undetermined condition is or is not fulfilled, then his decrees can neither be eternal nor immutable.

This latter paragraph is much clearer than the former. We may agree with the former that the decrees, including of course everything connected with the Atonement, are "rational determinations." By this phrase I understand that the whole plan of history is teleological. Prior events prepare for later events. Judas' betrayal prepared for the arrest and the crucifixion. But contrary to what Hodge says, this does not rule out "the doctrine of necessity." While one must reject the idea that there is any development in God there is indeed development in history. Nor is the word "mere" very clear, when Hodge says that God does not act by a mere necessity of nature. If the term *nature* is meant to indicate the physical universe, Mother Nature as some poets call it, and *natura naturans* as Spinoza said, of course we agree with Hodge's statement. Furthermore, Hodge's reference to

Spinoza seems to support the idea that he is thinking of the universe. Spinoza was a pantheist who frequently used the phrase *Deus sive Natura*. But Hodge seems to me to have confused Mother Nature with the nature of God. The important question is whether God acts necessarily by his own nature. Could God have willed to save no one? Could God have willed that Anthony should have been victorious, or that the Duc de Guise should have defeated Henry IV? If one says that the defeat of Anthony was necessitated, and that God could not have willed otherwise, it does not follow, as Hodge seems to say it does, that God would have acted without design. Nor does the doctrine of necessity require that God's intellectual force be analogous to the instincts of irrational animals. At best Hodge has in his attack on Spinozism used language that can be applied to views that are not at all Spinozistic. And one of these views is the Christian doctrine of God and his decrees.

One of the terms the Hodges use with confidence and satisfaction is *freedom*. God was free to create or not to create; God was free to save or not to save men; but if he freely chose to save any, he was necessitated to sacrifice Christ. In this he was not free. It is reasonable to suppose that this language somewhat reflects the discussions on the free will of man. At any rate, the idea of God's freedom should be clarified. Some types of freedom are obviously irrelevant to the present discussion: a man may be free from disease, free from prejudice, or free from his previous wife. Though these meanings are irrelevant, one notes that freedom is often, almost always, freedom *from* something.

Spinoza is an exception, for his freedom is a freedom *to*. A grain of wheat is free to grow, if it is planted in good soil rather than having fallen on a rock where a bird can pick it up. The bird is more free than a grain of wheat because, if this rock had no grain of wheat on it, the bird can fly and find food elsewhere.

A man is more free than a bird because he can survive in many more circumstances. Thus, Spinoza says, freedom is not the ability to do either of two things in the same circumstance, but the ability to do the same thing in many circumstances.

Arminian and Romish freedom is the power of contrary choice. There is nothing, absolutely nothing, in any circumstance, in heaven above, or earth beneath, or the waters under the earth, but especially in heaven above, that necessitates a given volition. The opposite choice is always as possible as the one chosen.

But what might divine freedom be? One thing is clear. There is no power, circumstance, or principle external to God that necessitates or even induces him to do anything. Of course, before the creation of the world there were no circumstances at all, though some philosopher might say that there were eternal principles external to him. But for the Christian there was nothing before he created something. But does this mean that God could have chosen not to create?

The confusion that permeates discussion on this subject arises from the rather natural impulse to understand the will of God as similar to the will of man, or, more accurately, similar to what many theologians think the will of man is. In particular, they picture God as earlier undecided, and later at a moment in time God makes a choice. The theologian may indeed recognize that there is no external motivation, but he still holds to the possibility that God could have willed otherwise.

This confusion is due to the fact that the authors often forget that God is immutable. Grotius seems to have argued that no one form of Atonement is absolutely necessary. The law, he maintains, is a product of the divine *will* and not something inherent in his nature. Therefore God is *free* to enforce, to abrogate, or in any way to alter the laws. Grotius is not the only one who seems to assume that God's will is *free* in the sense that he can change his mind at any time. Freedom, however, should be defined and the implications of the definition should be stated. For example, human freedom may consist in the circumstance that one's conduct is not determined by physico-chemical law. From this definition, if accepted, it follows that the universe is not a mechanism. But, so far as this definition goes, human conduct can be necessitated by a divine teleological law. As for the freedom of God, he is surely free from control by any superior power, for there is no power superior to God. But as immutable by nature—see Grotius's distinction between will and nature a few lines above—God's will and action are unalterable.

Hodge, who rejects Grotius's view of the Atonement, is perhaps a little, but not much, better. God, he says, "wills the precept *because* it is *intrinsically* right. . . . There must be an absolute standard of righteousness." Such a statement places a standard of justice outside of God. The standard is *intrinsically* right, hence independent of God's sovereignty—indeed, sovereignty has been abandoned. Hodge, however, wants to avoid this implication, for unlike Grotius, Hodge immediately adds, "This absolute standard is the divine nature . . . the divine intelligence" (*op. cit.*, p. 59). This addition gives the impression of maintaining divine sovereignty as against any external power or principle. But it faces an equally difficult objection. It raises the question as to the difference between will and nature. What is nature? Do we not speak of the nature of this or that? Then must we not speak of the nature of God, the nature of God's will, the nature of God's intelligence? Nature is not a constituent of anything. It is simply the thing's characteristics. God's nature, like a dog's nature, is such and such because such are the characteristics of the dog or of God. The nature is simply the way the dog or God acts. There is no *nature* that controls God's will. As Isaac Watts once wrote, "Dogs delight to bark and bite, for 'tis their nature to."[1]

In addition to examining the term *nature*, one must ask what is *will*? If we speak of the human will, we refer to a somewhat momentary act of choice. After having considered the relative desirability of this versus that line of action, or, what is the same thing, between an action and doing nothing, such as investing in A.T. & T. or just leaving the money in the checking account, and having puzzled over it indecisively for a period of time, we come to a conclusion and make our choice: We decide and do it. Then when we start to study theology and to consider the will of God, we are apt to think or subconsciously suppose that God makes decisions. He willed to create, he willed, after some deliberation, to save some, and so on. Though we may not say so out loud, we suppose that God was puzzled: He could create or he could refuse to create; he could or could refuse to save some; and if he decided to save some, he could use any means imaginable.

Now, although these choices are all of one nature, all subject to the same considerations, Hodge and others want to give the last question an answer different from their answer to the prior questions. This seems to me to be logically inconsistent, for if it relieves God of indecision on the last point, it pictures him as indecisive on the prior points, and assigns to him a relatively momentary act of choice. This makes God a temporal creature, or if not a creature, at least a temporal being.

Such a view is utterly inconsistent with divine omniscience. The immutable God never learned anything and never changed his mind. He knew everything from eternity. This *everything* includes both the number of mosquitoes in Jackson

---

1. The hymn, with animadversions on childhood, never became popular in the churches.

Hole and the number of planets in the solar system. Underlying these two examples is the creation of a temporal universe. For time began with the creation of the first non-omniscient angel.

Without claiming infallibility, and certainly not omniscience, yet I believe the above to be substantially what the Bible implies. Perhaps one should quote a few of the more clearly supporting verses. This is all the more appropriate because many, even most, of the volumes on Systematic Theology are strangely deficient at this point. Fortunately the indispensable Charnock fills the gap. Yet as Charnock shows, most of the Scriptural references are examples, rather than universal claims. If God knows the number of hairs on our heads and calls all the stars by name and notices the fall of every sparrow, we are encouraged to believe that he knows everything. There are none the less certain more general statements and inferences from his other attributes. Some of the latter will be quoted first.

The first of these verses is one that can easily be misunderstood, but neither should it be undervalued.

Psalm 147:5:	Great is our Lord, and of great power: his understanding is infinite.[1]
I Samuel 2:3:	. . . the Lord is a God of knowledge . . .
Colossians 2:3:	. . . in whom are hid all the treasures of wisdom and knowledge.

---

1. Though this verse helps to confirm God's omniscience, it must not be pressed too far. The Hebrew word does not mean *infinite*. In fact, Hebrew seems not to have any word meaning infinite. *Mispar*, the word in this verse, means a *number*. It can mean a small number or a large number. David sinfully wanted to know the relatively small number of his people. God knows the relatively large number of the stars. It is a delicate question whether God's knowledge is infinite in the English sense of the word. If it were, God's

These three, especially the latter two, are sufficiently universal and should, even by themselves, be considered conclusive. The next two might not seem universal by themselves, but it would be difficult to deny their implications.

Isaiah 46:10:   . . . Declaring the end from the beginning . . .

Hebrews 4:13:   There is no creature that is not manifest in his sight.

Could anyone be bold enough to assert that there are some non-creatures which might not be manifest in his sight? The following verses show that God's knowledge neither increases nor diminishes because he is immutable and eternal.

Exodus 3:14:   I am that I am.
Psalm 90:2:   . . . From everlasting to everlasting thou art God.
Malachi 3:6:   I am the Lord, I change not.
I Timothy 1:17:   . . . unto the King eternal . . .
James 1:17:   . . . the Father of lights with whom there is no variableness, nor shadow cast by turning.

Now come some verses that give examples, remarkable examples, of what God knows. Charnock cites dozens of such verses and expounds them all at length. Less than half a dozen

---

knowledge would be incomplete, if not unsystematic. The number of prime numbers equals the number of numbers because both are infinite; so that if God's knowledge were infinite, there would always be an extra item beyond the last. There would be no completeness. It is true that there can be an infinite "number" of propositions by counting the series: Today is Tuesday, it is true that today is Tuesday, it is true that it is true that today is Tuesday, *ad nauseam*.

should suffice here. They all tie in with the doctrine of the Atonement.

John 13:18:	I know whom I have chosen.
Romans 9:11:	The children being not yet born . . . that the purpose of God according to election might stand . . . .
Ephesians 1:4:	. . . chosen us in him before the foundation of the world . . . .
Ephesians 1:9:	. . . according to his good pleasure which he hath purposed in himself . . .
II Timothy 2:19:	. . . The Lord knoweth them that are his.

Notice that the first and fifth verses quoted, not to mention the others, make sense only if there are some whom God did not choose and are not his.

From the immutability and omniscience of God it follows necessarily that there is indeed no other possible method of salvation; not, however, for the reasons Hodge gives, but simply because of this immutability. In much of this discussion the authors speak as if God on one occasion produced an act of will and on another occasion he made another voluntary act. The Westminster Standards, however, reproduce the Biblical position that God is immutable. Therefore not only is the propitiatory method of atonement absolutely necessary, but also the number of mosquitoes in the world at any given instant. Every detail is a part of the all-comprehensive divine decree. God foreordains whatever comes to pass. Everything is necessary. This view exalts the Sovereignty of God. This view exalts God. Do not think that the reference to mosquitoes was flippant. William Cullen Bryant was no Calvinist and his theology is deplorable; yet on one occasion he stated the truth, even if he could not properly apply it to himself. A Christian can detach his lines from the Bryant theology and repeat with appreciation these words from *Lines to a Waterfowl*:

There is a Power whose care
Teaches thy way along that pathless coast,
The desert and illimitable air—
Lone wandering, but not lost.

He, who, from zone to zone,
Guides through the boundless sky thy certain flight,
In the long way that I must tread alone
Will lead my steps aright.

This settles the question as to whether the method of the Atonement is based on sovereignty or on justice, and the question whether God could have refused or neglected to save anybody. Not a chance. As previously asserted by the present writer, the sacrifice of Christ on the cross satisfied the justice of the Father. But now it should be clear that justice is one facet of sovereignty. There is no moral principle superior to God. I can say that there is no moral principle superior to the will of God. God's will and God's intellect are identical. Justice is what God thinks. To suppose that anything could have been otherwise is to suppose that God could have been otherwise than he is. The salvation of the elect is a part of the sovereign plan by which the universe goes on. God had to create—not because there was some power external to him, but because he is God. A God who might not create, or would not have created, is simply not the Biblical God.

In this twentieth century people like to be modern and up to date. Anything even ten years old, not to say two hundred or two thousand, is passé, benighted, medieval, stupid, unenlightened, erroneous, illogical, and just plain false. We today are educated. As one sweet little third-grader told her mother: I don't need to learn arithmetic; I'm developing a social consciousness. That is why Johnny can't read—theology.

Some Christians, *mirabile dictu* and *gloria in excelsis Deo*, still remember *Rock of Ages*. Of course they do not know that the author wrote on the present subject, any more than they know of his other 149 hymns. Here is something quite new and up to date, so far as the present generation is concerned.

Augustus Toplady wrote, among other things, *Observations on the Divine Attributes*.[1] The simplicity of God and the identity of all the divine attributes, used above to settle the relation between justice and sovereignty, Toplady expresses in the following words. "Although the great and ever blessed God is a Being absolutely simple . . . he is, nevertheless, in condescension to our weak and contracted faculties, represented in Scripture as possessed of divers properties, or attributes, which though seemingly different from his essence, are in reality essential to him, and constitutive of his very nature" (p. 675, col. 1). Toplady then specifies "his eternal wisdom, the absolute freedom and liberty of his will, the perpetuity and unchangeableness, both of himself and his decrees, his omnipotence, justice, and mercy."

The material is so good that it demands great restraint not to quote the entire article, twelve pages of long double columns. Fear not, modern reader, I shall give only a few short paragraphs.

> God is . . . so perfectly wise that nothing . . . can elude his knowledge . . . 'Known unto God are all his works from eternity.' Consequently God knows nothing . . . which he did not know and foresee from everlasting. . . . Whatever he foreknows

---

1. Pagination from *The Complete Works of Augustus M. Toplady*, London, 1869.

to be future shall necessarily and undoubtedly come to pass. For his knowledge can be no more frustated . . . than he can cease to be God. Nay, could either of these things be the case, he actually would cease to be God.

Some people argue that knowledge or foreknowledge does not necessitate anything. Even a man may know that an event will occur tomorrow, but this does not mean that he causes it to happen. Perhaps so. But if he does not cause it to happen, there must be some other cause which does, for unless it were certain, he could not know it.[1] Now, then, since omniscience shows that all events are certain, it follows that if God does not cause them, there must be a cause external to and independent of God. In other words, God has ceased to be God. Toplady recognizes this in this paragraph: "God's foreknowledge, taken abstractly, is not the sole cause of beings and events; but his will and foreknowledge together. Hence we find, Acts 2:23, that his determinate counsel and foreknowledge act in concert, the latter resulting from and being founded on, the former" (p. 675, col. 2).[2] Note that *foreknowledge* is dependent on determinate counsel. This is not true of a man. For example, I know that Christ will return. The event is determined, certain, and necessary. But I did not determine it.

Just a few more lines from Toplady: "Whatever comes to pass comes to pass by virtue of this absolute omnipotent will of

---

1. The illustration is faulty from the start because no man knows what will happen tomorrow.

2. I have not quoted an intervening paragraph which asserts that though man acts "from the first to the last moment of his life, in absolute subserviency . . . to the purposes and decrees of God concerning him; notwithstanding which he acts freely and voluntarily as if he was *sui juris*, . . . absolutely lord of himself." Translating this, and John Gill's term *coaction*, into twentieth century English, it means that man is free from the compulsion or "coaction" of physico-chemical mathematical equations. But that the will is not free from God, and that it is God who makes us willing, is stated in the Westminster Confession, X, i; compare IX, 3.

God, which is the primary and supreme cause of all things. . . .
The will of God is so the cause of all things as to be itself without
cause; for nothing can be the cause of that which is the cause of
everything" (p. 677, cols. 1, 2). Later in the volume (pp.
784-819, all double columns) there is his article *The Scheme of
Christian and Philosophical Necessity Asserted.*

In contrast with the types of interest prominent among the
relatively conservative Christians of the present day, those of an
earlier age can be instructive. William Cunningham, Professor
of Church History at New College, Edinburgh, recounts[1] an
interesting attack on Dr. Chalmers by Sir William Hamilton.
The latter denounced the former as a fatalist, a pantheist, and as
being ignorant and suicidal in theology. His reason was that
Chalmers taught the doctrine of philosophical necessity. Cunningham's conclusion was that the Westminster Confession
permits but does not teach philosophical necessity, that Chalmers not only was at liberty to accept that view, but that also his
orthodoxy was impeccable.

On a lower level, a much lower level, *The Presbyterian
Journal*, November 18, 1981, includes an article by the
Reverend Donald A. Dunkerley entitled *Hyper-Calvinism Today*. This author is to be highly commended because he knows
what hyper-calvinism is and he states the definition clearly.
Most popular writers and preachers neither state nor know it.
Hyper-calvinism is "that view of Calvinism which holds that
'there is no world-wide call to Christ sent out to all sinners,
neither are all men bidden to take him as their Savior.'
Hyper-calvinists . . . maintain that Christ should be held forth
or offered as Savior to those only whom God effectually calls"
(p. 14, col. 1).

---

1. *The Reformers and the Theology of the Reformation*; first published 1862; London
1967; pp. 471-524.

It seems that there are such people, people who are derisively called Hard-shell Baptists. There must be very few such, and I do not know of any Presbyterians who qualify. Dunkerley himself acknowledges that they are "an almost negligible minority."

Yet, though he knows very well what the term means, he wants to extend its pejorative overtones to people to whom the term does not apply. His method is to ask rhetorical questions which he wants his readers to answer in the affirmative, when clearly the correct answer is negative. In spite of his acknowledgment that hyper-calvinists are an almost negligible minority, and after describing various forms of evangelism, he complains that "we lack and urgently need in our day [a] compassionate evangelism." Well, this is true, but in its context it seems to mean that hyper-calvinism is almost the worst aberration of the twentieth century. Perhaps of the eighteenth century also, for Whitefield, whom he cites with approval, hardly evinces the evangelistic methods he seems to require.

Of course the Bible commands us to preach the gospel to all men. To a hyper-calvinist who insisted that a minister should preach the gospel only to the elect, Clarence Edward Macartney, if I remember correctly, replied, "You point out to me which persons are the elect and I shall confine my preaching to them."

But when Mr. Dunkerley wants to tell everyone that "God loves you," I wonder how he can defend that phrase when not only Jacob, but Esau also is in the audience.[1]

Such then is my view of sovereignty, and my replies to assorted objections. *Deo soli gloria.*

---

1. In the article it seems that the hyper-calvinist and Mr. Dunkerley misunderstand John 3:16, and that the latter's doctrine of assurance is at variance with the First Epistle of John.

19. The Extent of the Atonement

This concluding section could be written as somewhat of an anti-climax. All the important points have already been expounded, and of course they imply that Christ died specifically to save the elect and no others. Unless a person believes in universal salvation, he must believe that some are lost; and if some are lost, one can most reasonably suppose that many if not all who were drowned in the flood were lost; and surely many if not all who perished physically in the fire rained down on Sodom and Gomorrah also perished eternally. Given these assumptions one may ask, Did Christ, while on the cross, intend to save these people? Obviously not, for they were already in hell and there is no second chance. Thus from the consideration of many passages in Scripture we can infer that the extent or application of the Atonement is limited to the elect. All the doctrines of Scripture are logically interdependent. Since the most pertinent doctrines have already been discussed, any further appeal to Scriptural passages is anti-climactic and unnecessary.

However, this procedure, or lack of procedure, would incite the Arminians to a storm of protest. They would charge that we are substituting "mere human logic" for Scriptural revelation, and on a point where the Scriptures beyond all dispute emphatically support their view. Didn't God so love the world, every person in the world, that he wanted to save all? Furthermore, unlike the almost non-existent hyper-calvinism, Arminianism has numerous adherents in America. Without counting the Lutherans, who have similar views, at least on this particular subject, one surmises (since accurate statistics are not available) that Arminians form a large majority of so-called fundamentalists or evangelicals. Therefore those who understand the Scriptures must be constantly combatting Arminianism, for it is so widespread. Anyone who notes the actual procedures of evangelism in this country—some groups ignore both sin and repentance—can hardly ignore the vast difference between the preaching of various evangelists. A radio sermon the other day provided a somewhat amusing example. The preacher was making a certain point and refuting other possibilities. Possibility number one fails because verse so and so rules it out. Possibility number two collapses on these other verses. And possibility number three is simply Calvinism—period. What could possibly be more devastating? Thus the question is not limited to what some ignorant people call the dry bones of theology; it concerns the actual preaching, the actual message, of evangelists who are very much alive and present.

The main idea of Arminianism in connection with what Calvinists call Christ's Satisfaction is that Christ died in order, not to save some, but simply to make salvation possible to all. According to the theory, Christ died for all men *alike*, and not "specially of those who believe." The Father did not give to Christ a "peculiar people" or a "promised possession." Christ never procured reconciliation for anyone. But if so, how could Isaiah say, "He shall see his seed. . . . he shall see of the travail of his soul and shall be satisfied"? At any rate, according to the Arminians, Christ never actually procured the reconciliation of anyone: He merely removed the obstacle of divine justice so as to make all mankind salvable. The Atonement has no efficacy in itself so far as application goes. For that matter, on their theory, the ransom might not have released anyone. In other words, Christ did not intend to save anybody, nor did his death insure the salvation of anybody. Salvation is an additional work of man's free will. One man is more spiritual than another, or more clever, or more determined; and so of his own natural ability he takes advantage of the chance that Christ offered equally to all. If any person wishes to be reconciled to God, the man himself must do something of his own free will to produce the reconciliation. He must apply redemption to himself. Arminianism, as noted above, contradicts Calvinism at every point; and here we see it contradicting the obviously Biblical teaching that man is dead in sin. His will is not totally depraved; without regeneration he can exercise faith. Though no one accuses the Arminians of being Roman Catholics, the two agree on one point at least, a fatal point, namely, that while Christ's sacrifice was necessary for salvation, it is not *sufficient*. Man must add some meritorious work of his own.

To support the doctrine of the L in TULIP, Limited Atonement, it is sufficient to deduce it logically from other doctrines or other parts of the doctrine of the Atonement. But we are not unwilling to adduce Scriptural passages that more directly and explicitly assert it. First, however, a minor division of the subject.

The application or extent of redemption can be divided into two parts. The word *application* suggests some method of applying redemption; the word *extent* clearly refers to the number or identities of those who are saved. Redemption is applied by the Holy Spirit. He resurrects the sinner, dead in trespasses and sins, to newness of life. He changes a man's recalcitrant will into a believing will. He works faith in us. This part of God's plan is better discussed under the subject of the work of the Holy Spirit. Here we are more closely concerned with the *extent* of the application.

As for the Scriptural material, even the Arminians must admit that many verses have a bearing on several topics. An ordinary prophecy of a future event, such as the release of the Jews by Cyrus, supports the doctrine of omniscience, supports the view that Israel was a chosen nation, and teaches us something of how God uses civil rulers. Hence we cannot permit the Arminians to prohibit us from referring to the Covenant of Redemption (section three, above). The Father gave to his Son a certain number of people to redeem. This body of people is God's peculiar possession. It does not include everyone, for Jacob have I loved, but Esau have I hated. The not very bright preacher, quoted by Mr. Dunkerley, who found difficulty with John 3:16, probably had no greater problems with it than Mr. Dunkerley himself, for clearly he misinterprets it. Romans 9:13 should help them both.

Emphasizing the substitutionary nature of the Atonement, Smeaton (*op. cit.,* p. 174) says:

> The redemptive efficacy of his death is described as taking place within a given circle, and as bearing upon a given company of persons. . . . The Lord's sayings on this point are so express that we are not left in any doubt whatever that the atonement was offered specially for the persons who [actually] receive the benefit of his death. . . . Its extent coincides with its effects.

On the next page: "Our Lord calls the object of his atonement his sheep (John 10:15). . . . They are already called his sheep because they were given to him in the divine decree, and known as his own. . . . Christ did not die in a merely indeterminate way and in uncertainty whether he should have a flock, but with special objects of redemption [particular individuals] before his mind. . . . He died for the sheep," not for the wolves. Smeaton has several pages refuting Arminianism and Semi-Pelagian views.[1]

The crux of the matter lies in Christ's and the Father's

---

1. William Cunningham, *Historical Theology*, Banner of Truth Trust, 1960; Vol. II, pp. 237-370, gives a most detailed and almost fatiguing account of the Calvinistic view of the Atonement and follows it with 130 pages of argument against the Arminians.

intention. Did Christ intend to save some, or none? Did he
intend to save the Sodomites? What was his purpose? Two
verses from John's Gospel obviously bear on this intention.

| John 10:15: | . . . I lay down my life for the sheep. |
| John 17:9: | I pray not for the world. |

In answer to any Arminian or other sort of misinterpreta-
tion, let it be said that the intrinsic merit of Christ's sacrifice was
sufficient to buy the redemption of any or all. The question is,
Whom in particular did he actually buy? Three more verses
coincide in answering this question.

Acts 20:28:	. . . the church of God which he hath purchased with his own blood.
Romans 8:32-33:	. . . delivered him up for us all . . . God's elect.
Ephesians 5:25:	. . . as Christ also loved the church and gave himself for it.

If anyone says that while of course Christ died for the
sheep and the church, he also redeemed others, let such a one
quote the verse that says the Sodomites are now in heaven.
Since this obviously cannot be done, the Arminians use verses
of more general application.

| I Timothy 2:4,6: | Who will have all men to be saved and to come unto the knowledge of the truth . . . who gave himself a ransom for all. . . . |

Now, first, the context shows clearly enough that the two
words "all men" mean men of different social position and

different races: Gentiles as well as Jews, kings and other civil officers. In addition to the context the verses themselves clearly do not apply to every human individual singly. The verse says, "who will have all men . . . come to the knowledge of the truth." But God did not will to send preachers of the gospel to central Africa in the tenth century nor to the American Indians. The same is true of Europe and China in the tenth century before Christ. Hence "all men" in these verses do not mean every last human being who has ever lived.

In case anyone should want to reply that God really wanted to, but was prevented by some circumstance or other, the irrefragable answer is

Psalm 136:6:   Whatsoever the Lord pleased, that
                                did he in heaven, and in the earth, in
                                the seas, and all deep places.

We now pass to another phase of the same problem. If the Arminians and the Neo-orthodox accuse us of depending too much on logic and clear thinking, the Arminians also, if not the Neo-orthodox, sometimes depart from specific verses and try to deduce conclusions. They argue that only on the basis of a universal atonement can an evangelist offer salvation to all his audience and urge all to accept it. This is an attempt at logic, even if the attempt is poor. Some Baptists speak of the promiscuous preaching of the gospel; the Presbyterians usually use the term "the free offer of the gospel." Can such preaching occur on Calvinistic principles?

By the connotations of the English language the phrase "the free offer of the gospel" can be easily misunderstood. It sounds like "free will"—a doctrine both Calvin and Luther rejected.

The previous section on Sovereignty explained that God

was free from subjection to any external circumstance. Yet he is not free from himself. He cannot undeify himself. What then does the "free" offer of the gospel mean? Does it not mean that salvation is of grace and is free in the sense that we do not have to earn it, in fact cannot possibly earn it? This is indeed a sort of freedom, but hardly the free offer of the gospel.

Louis Berkhof (*op. cit.*, p. 397) gives a six part definition of the term: (1) the offer of salvation does not pretend to be a revelation of the secret counsel of God; (2) this offer is always conditioned by faith, a faith contingent upon the operation of the Holy Spirit; (3) this offer does not consist in the declaration that Christ made atonement for every man and really intends to save each one; (4) it is not the duty of the preacher to harmonize the secret counsel of God [as to which individuals will be saved] with his declarative will; (5) Dr. Shedd said that God may call upon the non-elect to do a thing that God delights in; and (6) the universal offer of salvation serves the purpose of disclosing the aversion and obstinacy of man; and if it were not made, sinners might say that they would have gladly accepted if it had been ofered to them.[1]

It seems to me that the phrase "the free offer of the gospel" is a poor one, especially since many, unlike Berkhof, make no attempt to explain it. The phrase "promiscuous preaching" might do, but perhaps the "unrestricted preaching of the gospel" would be better. Since the hyper-calvinists are so few in number, the strong emphasis on the "free offer of the gospel" is at best unneeded, and in my experience sometimes woefully misapplied. In one case it was misapplied to a person who did a fair amount of street preaching. In fact, since it is hardly possible, in fact impossible, to know that everyone in a

---

1. These six statements are verbatim, but omissions are not indicated by the usual three dots.

congregation is already regenerated, it is hard to guess where, on the hard-shell position, any gospel preaching could take place.

It should be obvious therefore that the "free offer of the gospel" is not at all inconsistent with the doctrine of the Limited Atonement. The former identifies the people to whom preachers should preach: everybody. The latter refers to the intention of Christ to redeem certain unnamed individuals. And that Christ did not intend to redeem everybody is sufficiently stated in the verses quoted and others. It is also validly deduced from the biblical position on the Sovereignty of God. Other biblical passages describe the means by which the Atonement was accomplished: federal headship and traducianism. More central are Satisfaction, Propitiation, and Expiation, each one a phase of the Vicarious Sacrifice. This sacrifice became possible through the Virgin Birth and Christ's active obedience, all of which go back to the Covenants of Grace, of Redemption, and thus again to the Sovereignty of God.

On one occasion, which I remember well, at a seminary service, several students, even advanced students, became vocally angry because I had preached that

It pleased God in his eternal purpose to ordain the Lord Jesus, his only begotten Son, to be the mediator between God and man . . . unto whom he did from all eternity give a people to be . . . redeemed. . . . The Lord Jesus by his perfect obedience and sacrifice of himself . . . hath fully satisfied the justice of his Father, and purchased . . . an everlasting inheritance . . . for all those whom the Father hath given unto him. . . . To all those for whom Christ hath purchased redemption, he doth certainly and effectually apply and communicate the same . . . effectually persuading them by his Spirit to believe and obey. . . .

That is the gospel, and it ought to be preached to all men.

Indices

Index

Scripture Index

159

Appendices

The Crisis of Our Time

Historians have christened the thirteenth century the Age of Faith and termed the eighteenth century the Age of Reason. The twentieth century has been called many things: the Atomic Age, the Age of Inflation, the Age of the Tyrant, the Age of Aquarius. But it deserves one name more than the others: the Age of Irrationalism. Contemporary secular intellectuals are anti-intellectual. Contemporary philosophers are anti-philosophy. Contemporary theologians are anti-theology.

In past centuries secular philosophers have generally believed that knowledge is possible to man. Consequently they expended a great deal of thought and effort trying to justify knowledge. In the twentieth century, however, the optimism of the secular philosophers has all but disappeared. They despair of knowledge.

Like their secular counterparts, the great theologians and doctors of the church taught that knowledge is possible to man. Yet the theologians of the twentieth century have repudiated that belief. They also despair of knowledge. This radical skepticism has filtered down from the philosophers and theologians and penetrated our entire culture, from television to music to literature. *The Christian in the twentieth century is confronted with an overwhelming cultural consensus—sometimes stated explicitly, but most often implicitly: Man does not and cannot know anything truly.*

167

What does this have to do with Christianity? Simply this: If man can know nothing truly, man can truly know nothing. We cannot know that the Bible is the Word of God, that Christ died for sin, or that Christ is alive today at the right hand of the Father. Unless knowledge is possible, Christianity is nonsensical, for it claims to be knowledge. What is at stake in the twentieth century is not simply a single doctrine, such as the Virgin Birth, or the existence of Hell, as important as those doctrines may be, but the whole of Christianity itself. If knowledge is not possible to man, it is worse than silly to argue points of doctrine—it is insane.

The irrationalism of the present age is so thorough-going and pervasive that even the Remnant—the segment of the professing church that remains faithful—has accepted much of it, frequently without even being aware of what it was accepting. In some circles this irrationalism has become synonymous with piety and humility, and those who oppose it are denounced as rationalists—as though to be logical were a sin. Our contemporary anti-theologians make a contradiction and call it a Mystery. The faithful ask for truth and are given Paradox. If any balk at swallowing the absurdities of the anti-theologians, they are frequently marked as heretics or schismatics who seek to act independently of God.

There is no greater threat facing the true Church of Christ at this moment than the irrationalism that now controls our entire culture. Communism, guilty of tens of millions of murders, including those of millions of Christians, is to be feared, but not nearly so much as the idea that we do not and cannot know the truth. Hedonism, the popular philosophy of America, is not to be feared so much as the belief that logic—that "mere human logic," to use the religious irrationalists' own phrase—is futile. The attacks on truth, on revelation, on the intellect, and on logic are renewed daily. But note well:

The misologists—the haters of logic—use logic to demonstrate the futility of using logic. The anti-intellectuals construct intricate intellectual arguments to prove the insufficiency of the intellect. The anti-theologians use the revealed Word of God to show that there can be no revealed Word of God—or that if there could, it would remain impenetrable darkness and Mystery to our finite minds.

Nonsense Has Come

Is it any wonder that the world is grasping at straws—the straws of experientialism, mysticism and drugs? After all, if people are told that the Bible contains insoluble mysteries, then is not a flight into mysticism to be expected? On what grounds can it be condemned? Certainly not on logical grounds or Biblical grounds, if logic is futile and the Bible unintelligible. Moreover, if it cannot be condemned on logical or Biblical grounds, it cannot be condemned at all. If people are going to have a religion of the mysterious, they will not adopt Christianity: They will have a genuine mystery religion. "Those who call for Nonsense," C.S. Lewis once wrote, "will find that it comes." And that is precisely what has happened. The popularity of Eastern mysticism, of drugs, and of religious experience is the logical consequence of the irrationalism of the twentieth century. There can and will be no Christian revival—and no reconstruction of society—unless and until the irrationalism of the age is totally repudiated by Christians.

The Church Defenseless

Yet how shall they do it? The spokesmen for Christianity have been fatally infected with irrationalism. The seminaries, which annually train thousands of men to teach millions of

Christians, are the finishing schools of irrationalism, completing the job begun by the government schools and colleges. Some of the pulpits of the most conservative churches (we are not speaking of the apostate churches) are occupied by graduates of the anti-theological schools. These products of modern anti-theological education, when asked to give a reason for the hope that is in them, can generally respond with only the intellectual analogue of a shrug—a mumble about Mystery. They have not grasped—and therefore cannot teach those for whom they are responsible—the first truth: "And ye shall know the truth." Many, in fact, explicitly deny it, saying that, at best, we possess only "pointers" to the truth, or something "similar" to the truth, a mere analogy. Is the impotence of the Christian Church a puzzle? Is the fascination with Pentecostalism and faith healing among members of conservative churches an enigma? Not when one understands the sort of studied nonsense that is purveyed in the name of God in the seminaries.

The Trinity Foundation

The creators of The Trinity Foundation firmly believe that theology is too important to be left to the licensed theologians—the graduates of the schools of theology. They have created The Trinity Foundation for the express purpose of teaching the faithful all that the Scriptures contain—not warmed over, baptized, secular philosophies. Each member of the board of directors of The Trinity Foundation has signed this oath: "I believe that the Bible alone and the Bible in its entirety is the Word of God and, therefore, inerrant in the autographs. I believe that the system of truth presented in the Bible is best summarized in the Westminster Confession of Faith. So help me God."

The ministry of The Trinity Foundation is the presentation of the system of truth taught in Scripture as clearly and as completely as possible. We do not regard obscurity as a virtue, nor confusion as a sign of spirituality. Confusion, like all error, is sin, and teaching that confusion is all that Christians can hope for is doubly sin.

The presentation of the truth of Scripture necessarily involves the rejection of error. The Foundation has exposed and will continue to expose the irrationalism of the twentieth century, whether its current spokesman be an existentialist philosopher or a professed Reformed theologian. We oppose anti-intellectualism, whether it be espoused by a neo-orthodox theologian or a fundamentalist evangelist. We reject misology, whether it be on the lips of a neo-evangelical or those of a Roman Catholic charismatic. To each error we bring the brilliant light of Scripture, proving all things, and holding fast to that which is true.

The Primacy of Theory

The ministry of The Trinity Foundation is not a "practical" ministry. If you are a pastor, we will not enlighten you on how to organize an ecumenical prayer meeting in your community or how to double church attendance in a year. If you are a homemaker, you will have to read elsewhere to find out how to become a total woman. If you are a businessman, we will not tell you how to develop a social conscience. The professing church is drowning in such "practical" advice.

The Trinity Foundation is unapologetically theoretical in its outlook, believing that theory without practice is dead, and that practice without theory is blind. The trouble with the professing church is not primarily in its practice, but in its theory. Christians do not know, and many do not even care to know, the doctrines of Scripture. Doctrine is intellectual, and Christians are generally anti-intellectual. Doctrine is ivory tower philosophy, and they scorn ivory towers. The ivory tower, however, is the control tower of a civilization. It is a fundamental, theoretical mistake of the practical men to think that they can be merely practical, for practice is always the practice of some theory. The relationship between theory and practice is the relationship between cause and effect. If a person believes correct theory, his practice will tend to be correct. The practice of contemporary Christians is immoral because it is the practice of false theories. It is a major theoretical mistake of the practical men to think that they can ignore the ivory towers of the philosophers and theologians as irrelevant to their lives. Every action that the "practical" men take is governed by the thinking that has occurred in some ivory tower—whether that tower be the British Museum, the Academy, a home in Basel, Switzerland, or a tent in Israel.

In Understanding Be Men

It is the first duty of the Christian to understand correct theory—correct doctrine—and thereby implement correct practice. This order—first theory, then practice—is both logical and Biblical. It is, for example, exhibited in Paul's epistle to the Romans, in which he spends the first eleven chapters expounding theory and the last five discussing practice. The contemporary teachers of Christians have not only reversed the order, they have inverted the Pauline emphasis on theory and practice. The virtually complete failure of the teachers of the professing church to instruct the faithful in correct doctrine is the cause of the misconduct and cultural impotence of Christians. The Church's lack of power is the result of its lack of truth. The *gospel* is the power of God, not religious experience or personal relationship. The Church has no power because it has abandoned the gospel, the good news, for a religion of experientialism. Twentieth century American Christians are children carried about by every wind of doctrine, not knowing what they believe, or even if they believe anything for certain.

The chief purpose of The Trinity Foundation is to counteract the irrationalism of the age and to expose the errors of the teachers of the church. Our emphasis—on the Bible as the sole source of truth, on the primacy of the intellect, on the supreme importance of correct doctrine, and on the necessity for systematic and logical thinking—is almost unique in Christendom. To the extent that the church survives—and she will survive and flourish—it will be because of her increasing acceptance of these basic ideas and their logical implications.

We believe that the Trinity Foundation is filling a vacuum in Christendom. We are saying that Christianity is intellectually defensible—that, in fact, it is the only intellectually defensible system of thought. We are saying that God has made the wisdom of this world—whether that wisdom be called science, religion, philosophy, or common sense—foolishness. We are appealing to all Christians who have not conceded defeat in the intellectual battle with the world to join us in our efforts to raise a standard to which all men of sound mind can repair.

The love of truth, of God's Word, has all but disappeared in our time. We are committed to and pray for a great instauration. But though we may not see this reformation of Christendom in our lifetimes, we believe it is our duty to present the whole counsel of God because Christ has commanded it. The results of our teaching are in God's hands, not ours. Whatever those results, His Word is never taught in vain, but always accomplishes the result that He intended it to accomplish. Professor Gordon H. Clark has stated our view well:

There have been times in the history of God's people, for example, in the days of Jeremiah, when refreshing grace and widespread revival were not to be expected: the time was one of chastisement. If this twentieth century is of a similar nature, individual Christians here and there can find comfort and strength in a study of God's Word. But if God has decreed happier days for us and if we may expect a world-shaking and genuine spiritual awakening, then it is the author's belief that a zeal for souls, however necessary, is not the sufficient condition. Have there not been devout saints in every age, numerous enough to carry on a revival? Twelve such persons are plenty. What distinguishes the arid ages from the period of the Reformation, when nations were moved as they had not been since Paul preached in Ephesus, Corinth, and Rome, is the latter's fullness of knowledge of God's Word. To echo an early Reformation thought, when the ploughman and the garage attendant know the Bible as well as the theologian does, and know it better than some contemporary theologians, then the desired awakening shall have already occurred.

In addition to publishing books, of which *The Atonement* is the seventeenth, the Foundation publishes a bimonthly newsletter, *The Trinity Review*. Subscriptions to *The Review* are free; please write to the address below to become a subscriber. If you would like further information or would like to join us in our work, please let us know.

The Trinity Foundation is a non-profit foundation tax-exempt under section 501 (c) (3) of the Internal Revenue Code of 1954. You can help us disseminate the Word of God through your tax-deductible contributions to the Foundation.

And we know that the Son of God is come, and hath given us an understanding, that we may know him that is true, and we are in him that is true, in his Son Jesus Christ. This is the true God, and eternal life.

John W. Robbins
President

Intellectual Ammunition

The Trinity Foundation is committed to the reconstruction of philosophy and theology along Biblical lines. We regard God's command to bring all our thoughts into conformity with Christ very seriously, and the books listed below are designed to accomplish that goal. They are written with two subordinate purposes: (1) to demolish all secular claims to knowledge; and (2) to build a system of truth based upon the Bible alone.

Works of Philosophy

Answer to Ayn Rand, John W. Robbins $4.95
  The only analysis and criticism of the views of novelist-philosopher Ayn Rand from a consistently Christian perspective.

Behaviorism and Christianity, Gordon H. Clark $5.95
  Behaviorism *is a critique of both secular and religious behaviorists. It includes chapters on John Watson, Edgar A. Singer Jr., Gilbert Ryle, B.F. Skinner, and Donald MacKay. Clark's refutation of behaviorism and his argument for a Christian doctrine of man are unanswerable.*

177

A Christian View of Men and Things, Gordon H. Clark $8.95
   No other book achieves what A Christian View *does: the presentation of Christianity as it applies to history, politics, ethics, science, religion, and epistemology. Clark's command of both worldly philosophy and Scripture is evident on every page, and the result is a breathtaking and invigorating challenge to the wisdom of this world.*

Clark Speaks From The Grave, Gordon H. Clark $3.95
   Dr. Clark chides some of his critics for their failure to defend Christianity competently. Clark Speaks *is a stimulating and illuminating discussion of the errors of contemporary apologists.*

John Dewey, Gordon H. Clark $2.00
   Dewey had has an immense influence on American philosophy and education. His irrationalism, the effects of which we can see in government education, is thoroughly criticized by Dr. Clark.

Language and Theology, Gordon H. Clark $4.95
   Many philosophers and theologians believe language is a barrier to communication, not an aid. For those who believe in the Word of God, such a view is anathema. Clark analyzes and refutes the language theories of secular and religious philosophers: Bertrand Russell, Ludwig Wittgenstein, Rudolf Carnap, A.J. Ayer, Herbert Feigl, Wilbur Marshall Urban, E.L. Mascall, Horace Bushnell, Langdon Gilkey, William Hordern, and Kenneth Hamilton.

Logic, Gordon H. Clark $8.95
   Written as a textbook for Christian schools, Logic *is another unique book from Clark's pen. His presentation of the laws of thought, which must be followed if Scripture is to be understood correctly, and which are found in Scripture itself, is both clear and thorough.* Logic *is an indispensable book for the thinking Christian.*

Religion, Reason and Revelation, Gordon H. Clark $7.95
   One of Clark's apological masterpieces, Religion, Reason and Revelation *has been praised for the clarity of its thought and language. It*

includes chapters on Is Christianity a Religion? Faith and Reason, Inspiration and Language, Revelation and Morality, and God and Evil. It is must reading for all serious Christians.

William James, Gordon H. Clark $2.00
    American philosophers are not that numerous, and Clark tackles and destroys two of the most influential: Dewey and James.

Works of Theology

The Atonement, Gordon H. Clark $8.95
    The Atonement *is easily one of the best, if not the best, explanations of the saving work of Christ that has yet been written. Dr. Clark takes the reader step-by-logical-step through the complexities of the Biblical teaching, and concludes with a summary that displays how the Biblical propositions fit neatly together into one system of truth. This is one of the major portions of his work on Systematic Theology.*

The Biblical Doctrine of Man, Gordon H. Clark $5.95
    Is man soul and body or soul, spirit, and body? What is the image of God? Is Adam's sin imputed to his children? Is evolution true? Are men totally depraved? What is the heart? These are some of the questions discussed and answered from Scripture in this book.

Biblical Predestination, Gordon H. Clark $4.95
    Clark thoroughly discusses one of the most controversial and pervasive doctrines of the Bible: that God is, quite literally, Almighty. Free will, the origin of evil, God's omniscience, creation, and the new birth are all presented within a Scriptural framework. The objections of those who do not believe in the Almighty God are considered and refuted.

Cornelius Van Til: The Man and The Myth $2.45
John W. Robbins
    The actual teachings of this eminent Philadelphia theologian have

been obscured by the myths that surround him. This book penetrates those myths and criticizes Van Til's surprisingly unorthodox views of God and the Bible.

Faith and Saving Faith, Gordon H. Clark $5.95
The views of the Roman Catholic church, John Calvin, Thomas Manton, John Owen, Charles Hodge, and B.B. Warfield are discussed in this book. Is the object of faith a person or a proposition? Is faith more than belief? Is belief more than thinking with assent, as Augustine said? In a world chaotic with differing views of faith, Clark clearly explains the Biblical view of faith and saving faith.

God's Hammer: The Bible and Its Critics, Gordon H. Clark $6.95
The starting point of Christianity, the doctrine on which all other doctrines depend, is "The Bible is the Word of God, and therefore inerrant in the autographs." Over the centuries the opponents of Christianity, with Satanic shrewdness, have concentrated their attacks on the truthfulness of the Bible. In the twentieth century the attack is not so much in the fields of history and archaeology as in philosophy. Clark's brilliant defense of the complete truthfulness of the Bible is captured in this collection of eleven major essays.

In Defense of Theology, Gordon H. Clark $12.95
There are four groups to whom Clark addresses this book: the average Christians who are uninterested in theology, the atheists and agnostics, the religious experientialists, and the serious Christians. The vindication of the knowledge of God against the objections of three of these groups is the first step in theology.

Logical Criticisms of Textual Criticism, Gordon H. Clark $2.95
In this critique of the science of textual criticism, Dr. Clark exposes the fallacious argumentation of the modern textual critics and defends the view that the early Christians knew better than the modern critics which manuscripts of the New Testament were more accurate.

Scripture Twisting in the Seminaries. Part 1: Feminism $5.95
John W. Robbins
   An analysis of the views of three graduates of Westminster Seminary on the role of women in the church.

The Trinity, Gordon H. Clark $8.95
   Apart from the doctrine of Scripture, no teaching of the Bible is more important than the doctrine of God. Clark's defense of the orthodox doctrine of the Trinity is a principal portion of a major new work of Systematic Theology now in progress. There are chapters on the deity of Christ, Augustine, the incomprehensibility of God, Bavinck and Van Til, and the Holy Spirit, among others.

What Do Presbyterians Believe? Gordon H. Clark $6.95
   This classic introduction to Christian doctrine has been republished. It is the best commentary on the Westminster Confession of Faith that has ever been written.

Commentaries on the New Testament

Ephesians, Gordon H. Clark $8.95
First and Second Thessalonians, Gordon H. Clark $5.95
The Pastoral Epistles (I and II Timothy and Titus) $9.95
   Gordon H. Clark
   All of Clark's commentaries are expository, not technical, and are written for the Christian layman. His purpose is to explain the text clearly and accurately so that the Word of God will be thoroughly known by every Christian. Revivals of Christianity come only through the spread of God's truth. The sound exposition of the Bible, through preaching and through commentaries on Scripture, is the only method of spreading that truth.

The Trinity Library

We will send you one copy of each of the 23 books listed above for the low price of $100. The regular price of these books is $147. Or you may order the books you want individually on the order blank at the back. Because some of the books are in short supply, we must reserve the right to substitute others of equal or greater value in The Trinity Library.

Thank you for your attention. We hope to hear from you soon. This special offer expires June 30, 1988. Foreign orders please include 20% for shipping.

Order Form

Name _____

Address _____

_____

Please: □ add my name to the mailing list for *The Trinity Review*. I
          understand that there is no charge for the *Review*.

□ accept my tax deductible contribution of $ _____
   for the work of the Foundation.

□ send me _____ copies of *The Atonement.* I enclose as
   payment $_____.

□ send me the Trinity Library of 23 books. I enclose $100 as
   full payment for it.

□ send me the following books. I enclose full payment in the
   amount of $_____ for them.

_____

_____

_____

_____

_____

_____

_____

Mail to: The Trinity Foundation
                  Post Office Box 169
                  Jefferson, MD 21755

Please add $1.00 for postage on orders less than $10. Thank you.
For quantity discounts, please write to the Foundation.